# THE DISHWASHER KING

JONATHAN DAY

ARTISTS GATE
PRESS

*To the sorceresses who bring magic to my life:*
*Nina, Julia, Sophia, Marea, Simona, and Osa*

New York City,
Present Day

# CHAPTER 1

IN HIS DREAMS, he never became a dishwasher.

Art Penn dreamed bigger than scrubbing pots and plates with steam swirling around him, sweat dripping into his eyes for nine hours a day. An hour after strapping on a thick rubber apron at an Upper Manhattan diner and setting to cleaning, his thick, muscular back began to ache and continued to nag him until the end of his shift. The ratty smell from the garbage can where he scraped uneaten food turned his stomach. Harsh soap and piping-hot water cracked the skin on his hands until they bled. As much as the teenager hated the work, he was never late, careless, or indifferent. No egg-encrusted plate or sauce-burned pot escaped his sink until it was spotless. Music helped ease the monotony, especially traditional English folk songs. Today, he listened on earbuds with the volume cranked up.

Over the music and roar of a dishwasher, he heard someone calling his name and turned around. The identical twin short-order cooks, wearing bandannas adorned with skulls and crossbones, pointed toward the food pass-through and raised their fists. A fight. Were Nikos or Tiny Toni in trouble? Art pulled out his earbuds and dashed through the swinging doors from the kitchen into the seating area. His boss, Nikos, had blocked the exit with his wheelchair to prevent a Herculean customer with a shaved, bullet-shaped head from leaving without paying for his breakfast.

"$17.40 cash money," Nikos demanded in a thick foreign accent.

Bullethead wiped yolk off the side of his mouth with a baseball-mitt-sized hand. "The eggs were rotten and the bread was moldy, you dumb Greek."

Without hesitation, Art jumped between them, standing toe to toe with a man ten years older, eight inches taller, and one hundred pounds heavier. "It'd be better for you to pay for what you ate," Art said. "You don't want to fight me."

If the dishwasher was scared, it didn't show in the icy calm in his eyes, one green and one blue. That lack of fear and the angry twitching of his forearm muscles unnerved the much bigger man, who swallowed hard. Poking a thick finger into Art's apron, he said without conviction, "A threat from a dishwasher doesn't make me shit my pants. Move."

Art stood his ground, and there was a tense silence as Bullethead didn't reach for his wallet. Customers at the counter and booths stopped eating, some with anxious looks. It appeared that the smaller dishwasher would be beaten to a pulp if this confrontation escalated. The waitress, Tiny Toni, pulled a wooden club almost as big as she was out from behind the counter, and she'd have no problem using it on the man who stiffed her for a tip.

"Step back, Art," Nikos said, breaking the tension. "You don't need no more police trouble by getting into another yarn ball." Then with a damning insult from his native country, he muttered, "Take the road, chicken thief!"

When Bullethead pushed Art aside, he made a big mistake. Shoving him was the least of it. By not paying, Bullethead had violated Art's unyielding belief in justice and respect. Art darted out to the sidewalk to block the thief's way, knowing he might have to take a punch or two. "I need you to not steal from my boss. Nikos let you slide. But now it's just you and me."

"You ain't gettin' paid enough to fight for a freakin' foreigner," Bullethead growled as he tried to walk around Art, but the teenager again blocked his exit. Without warning, the bigger man attempted to sucker punch Art, but the teenager deftly dodged the huge fist, his arms dangling loosely at his sides.

"Oh, a killer kung fu fighter?" Bullethead threw an uppercut. Art stepped backward, then pivoted on his left leg, spinning counter-clockwise in a complete circle. At the same time, he leaped, kicking Bullethead's right temple with such force that the giant dropped like a bag of stones.

"Not kung fu—karate," Art said, holding out his hand. "$17.40 cash money."

Bullethead pulled a twenty-dollar bill from his pocket. The teen-ager took it, then extended his hand again.

"And a tip for Toni." Out came another twenty. "Come back real soon to enjoy our special hospitality," Art said.

When he returned to the diner, everyone cheered like he'd won a boxing championship. But Art didn't feel the thrill of victory. Handing the money to Nikos gave him a sense of satisfaction that he could show some gratitude to his boss, who'd given a job to a homeless kid with a troubled past when nobody else would.

*Near the pond by Belvedere Castle* in Central Park, a boy with bangs hanging over his round glasses was reading a *Harry Potter* novel when a ball of light streaked across the sky and crashed onto the grass. An ancient-looking man with a long white beard, flowing robes, and a peaked hat emerged from the brightness. Next to him was a broad-shouldered teenager wearing chain-mail armor like a medieval warrior. "A wizard and a knight? No way!" the boy whispered.

Sitting near a stroller with a sleeping infant, his mother was too engrossed in her phone to look up.

The wizard looked around and muttered, "Whoops!"

The knight's eyes narrowed. "Est this not the place nor the century where thou brought infant Arthur?"

"The king lives with a family in the part of New York City called Queens. We've landed in Manhattan."

The boy was about to tell his mother that a wizard and a knight had just dropped from the sky but hesitated. She'd dismiss this information as another of his fantasies. So he just grinned to himself, reassured that there was magic in the world.

Two uniformed police officers on motor scooters rode toward the old man and the knight. "Behold, Merlin," the knight said. "Magical carts."

The officers stopped, and the one with a thick mustache said, "What was that flash of light? You guys got illegal fireworks?"

Merlin pointed to a mirror attached to his robe. "Most likely sunlight reflecting off this."

The police officers shared a skeptical look, then Mustache's partner said, "That sword better be a prop, Mack."

The knight put his hand on the weapon's hilt. "I knoweth not this Mack. I est Sir Lancelot of the Lake and quest my king to escort him to Camelot."

"We're really into our role, aren't we?" Mustache said, pointing. "The other Shakespeare in the Park actors are ... afar." He pointed to the open-air Delacorte Theater where men dressed in medieval costumes were theatrically bashing each other with prop swords while an actress with flowing strawberry-blonde hair in a period dress loudly rooted them on.

Merlin stared at the actress for a long moment, then shook his head. "It can't be her."

To Lancelot, this world Merlin had time-traveled him to was not dissimilar from seventh-century Camelot. The green expanse of the Great Lawn was like his jousting fields. The birds sounded the same. There was a castle, although smaller and less secure than the fortresses in England. The towering buildings surrounding this countryside had walls with unbarred windows covered with glass. Maybe there were no threats from rivals or uncivilized tribes from the North. But the clothes the natives wore were far less modest than what the maidens wore in his time, especially the young women facing the sun on this hot summer day—colorful fabric barely covering their chests and waists.

Merlin led Lancelot out of the park to a busy street where alien sights and sounds assaulted him. Hurtling metal boxes moved without being pulled by horses or oxen. Wagons as big as houses loudly accelerated. Two-wheeled magical carts growled like wild animals.

In the chaos and death of battle, he'd never experienced fear. It unnerved him that the sights he'd never seen and the sounds he'd never heard in this strange unknown world made his stomach churn and his palms sweat. "How can this raucous place and the twenty-first century be safe for our king?"

Merlin ignored the question and raised his arm to hail a taxi. But no drivers stopped when they saw an eccentric in flowing robes covered with crescent moons, birds' feet, and actual plants, and another guy with a three-foot-long sword. Finally, a huge, dent-scarred SUV with blistered black paint skidded to a stop. Merlin hesitated, and the driver rolled down the passenger side window. "The yellow cabs blew right by you, pal. So it's me, or you hoof it."

Merlin slid into the backseat, but the graceful knight struggled to fit his sword through the door. The driver adjusted his CATS *the Musical* baseball hat. "Where's the Renaissance Fair?"

"845 Kessler Street in Forest Hills, in the borough of Queens," Merlin said.

"Got it," the driver said as he picked up an instant camera from the seat next to him and took photos of Merlin and Lancelot. "You guys just made Geoffrey's celebrity photo album. I got maybe a thousand snaps of celebs, billionaires, and oddballs ... present company excluded." Then he stomped his foot on the gas, throwing his baffled passengers to the back of their seats. "How doth thou know the customs and the way they speaketh?" Lancelot asked.

"When I brought infant Arthur here seventeen years ago, I was fascinated by the magic these future people had created. I stayed for several months."

The SUV cruised by the main New York City library with two lion statues at the entrance. "I read a wealth of science books there, studied the moderns' powers, and learned how they talk and act." Merlin held up a credit card. "This has coinage inside."

As the SUV sped through Midtown, Lancelot stared blankly at the gigantic glass-and-steel buildings, and the roads covered with smooth black stone. In the English countryside, he was never lost. He knew how to use the sun to tell direction. Even on unmarked dirt paths, he could find his way. But in this maze, he feared he'd never find the entrance or the exit to safety. Thankfully, Merlin had promised they would locate Arthur and travel back to Camelot with him when a celestial event occurred at sunset that evening.

Seeing well-fed and finely tailored citizens hurrying along the side of the road and fabulous buildings that touched the clouds delighted Merlin. Only generations of peace could produce such a glorious civilization.

In England in 773, the false queen Morgan Le Fay had seized the throne and ruled with the edge of a sword as she dragged the country back into the Dark Ages, where fear and superstition reigned. Forces opposed to her tyranny fought back, and a brutal civil war raged with numerous military and civilian casualties.

Merlin knew only young King Arthur could rally the opposition to defeat Morgan and restore peace and prosperity in ancient Camelot. The wizard searched his many pockets until he found a signet ring that ancient kings used to press into hot wax to seal official royal documents. The ring had been passed to succeeding monarchs in Camelot for centuries, and now belonged to Arthur. *Do I hold the future of civilization in my hand?*

# CHAPTER 2

MERLIN ASKED THE DRIVER to wait, and he and
Lancelot stepped out of the SUV by a brick house in a neighborhood
of modest single-family homes.

"'Tis not a dwelling fit for our king," Lancelot said.

"The man who lives here has direct bloodlines to the Pendragon
family. But as you can see, the authority and grandeur of royalty have
diminished. Long ago, they shortened the name to Penn."

Merlin rang the doorbell, and a middle-aged man wearing a Mets
baseball jersey hanging over his potbelly opened the door. "You're too
late. The kid's gone."

"You accepted the responsibility and money to care for him,"
Merlin said.

"He was nothing but trouble. Always getting into fights to protect
some old lady or a nerd being bullied at school. I don't know how many

times I had to drive to the precinct to make excuses for him. He never learned, so I told him to get his ass out of my house."

Merlin's eyes glowed with rage. "Where can I find him?"

"He came back for his stupid karate medal and had on a Nikos' Diner T-shirt covered with stains. I guess he's washing dishes there. A suitable job for the thickheaded punk." Then, he slammed the door.

Lancelot put his hand on his sword. "I shalt slay him."

"Things are a little different in modern times, Sir Knight. We can't just kill those who annoy us."

Merlin walked to the SUV. "We need to go to Nikos' Diner."

"For sure. I stuck around 'cause I figured your guy wouldn't be home. Not many kings in Queens," the driver joked. "So where's this joint?" Reacting to the blank stares, he deliberately said, "Where's Nikos' Di-ner?"

"Est there more than one?" the knight asked.

"You guys really are from out of town. There are maybe a gazillion diners in the Big Apple, and most of them are run by Greeks. But not to worry." He searched on his phone. "I'm Geoffrey, and I'm a problem-solver."

*Geoffrey cruised slowly along Broadway* in the Washington Heights section of Upper Manhattan and finally stopped in front of Nikos' Diner. Merlin and Lancelot went inside. Customers sat by themselves, perusing their phones. Nikos was counting the morning's take at an antique cash register, and when he looked up to see two men in medieval outfits, he grinned. "Plenty of space at the counter or the booths," he said. "Your choice."

"Is there a seventeen-year-old young man here with one blue eye and one green eye?" Merlin asked.

Nikos's smile disappeared. "Who asks?"

"We've come from a distant place to bring him news about his family."

While the reason for their costumes was puzzling, their motive seemed nonthreatening. "Art's on break out back. You'll have to walk around."

*Overflowing trash cans* and open dumpsters lined the narrow alley at the rear of the diner.

Tiny Toni was leaning against a brick wall adorned with a Caribbean tropical paradise graffiti mural watching Art do rapid push-ups on the pavement. He counted, "99, 100," then jumped to his feet, wiping his hands to remove the street crud.

"You wash those pots like you're trying out for the dishwasher Olympics, and then you come out here and do all those things?" Toni wondered.

Art was a little winded and panted as he said, "I want to be ready."

She took a long puff on her unfiltered cigarette. "For what?"

"I don't know ... but something more challenging than washing dishes, for sure."

She dropped her cigarette and ground it out with her high-top sneaker. "I used to be ready." Then she went inside.

Among the rubbish, Art found a couple of gallon paint cans to use as weights and started doing curls as two men entered the alley. After he got kicked out of his foster home, Art survived on the streets for months and developed an almost feral wariness about strangers' potential for violence. The old man in the flowing robes with a peaked cap and waist-length white beard seemed harmless enough. But the tall, broad-shouldered teenager beside him was certainly dressed for a fight in armor with a sword at his side. He could be a hard case if things turned nasty. Art put the can down, shifted his weight to the balls of his feet, and let his arms dangle loosely at his sides, just in case.

The wizard came close and bowed his head toward Art. "Your Majesty."

But Lancelot didn't. How could this kid standing amid trash and wearing a kitchen maid's apron, pants that exposed his hairy shins, and a dirty white peasant shirt be his king? Merlin projected a thought in the knight's brain. *Forget the clothes. The blue and green eyes are proof of who he is. Believe and bow!* Merlin had been the knight's tutor since childhood and was never wrong. So Lancelot lowered his head, but not much.

Art eyed them suspiciously. "What do you guys want?"

"My name is Merlin, and this is Sir Lancelot. We bring you sad news. Your father, King Uther Pendragon, has died."

"Thou art the son of King Uther and now the ruler of all England," Lancelot said.

"You're pranking me, and it ain't making me laugh. I'm no Pendragon. I'm Art Penn, and the only thing I rule is a kitchen sink."

"Why doth thou not believe? A knight speaketh only the truth."

Art shot Lancelot a look: *Are you serious?*

"Open your mind ..." Merlin said.

But Art just turned to go inside. Merlin pointed a finger, lifting Art into the air. *Whoa!* The teenager looked down, and his feet were actually off the ground. He was floating. *What the ef?* His breathing got rapid, and his mouth became dry. He put his fists up, ready to fight. Judging from the kindly smile on the old man's face, though, Art sensed this Merlin character was probably not attacking. But suspended in the air, the feeling of powerlessness made him experience an anxiety he had never felt, even when attacked by street punks armed with knives.

The wizard lowered his finger, and Art gently returned to earth. A few deep breaths didn't calm him. "Who are you?" Art asked, his voice cracking.

"We traveled through time from the seventh century to bring you back to your home, to Camelot," Merlin said.

With his feet on solid ground, Art became bolder. "You guys've been smoking too much weed."

"Every night," Merlin continued, "you dream you're a warrior in armor at the head of a vast army. Your battle flag is decorated with an eagle's head and wings and a lion's hindquarters."

*He can't know my dream.* "A lot of little kids dream they're knights."

"Bright red masks cover the faces of the enemy soldiers. Atop a dark horse, their leader's covered in black armor. You march forward to fight, but this is where you always wake up. The battle never has a conclusion."

*I've never told that dream to anyone.*

Merlin flashed another smile. "And you have a birthmark shaped like a crescent moon on the sole of your left foot."

*Only Kate knows that! Who are these guys?*

"In Camelot, you'll do more good for more people than any king before and most who come after you," Merlin said. "Open your mind to hear and believe what I'm telling you, Arthur."

He had never been so confused. Ever. Did he really float, or was that a hallucination? Art's foster parents had kept the truth about his birth parents secret, but this stuff about his father being a king was completely wacko. *Get away from these nut cases now!* "I'm outta here."

Merlin pointed an arthritic-bent finger. "You cannot flee from your future."


*That evening, Art bounded out* of the youth shelter in Harlem, his dark-brown hair still wet from the shower he'd needed to wash off the kitchen grease and stink. He jogged three short blocks to the Meer, a pond at the north end of Central Park, and headed into the North Woods. On the internet, he'd discovered that the park was modeled on the Adirondack Mountains hundreds of miles north of the city. It was a miniature wilderness, and it soothed him. The farther he got from the shelter and soul-bruising tedium of washing dishes, the more his stride became energized.

He left the trail, scurried up a slope, and then pushed through shrubs into a clearing. Resting on the moss-covered ground, seventeen-year-old Kate Cambridge was reading an organic chemistry text and slammed the book shut with a mischievous smile when she saw him. Early-evening-slanting sunlight highlighted her blonde hair, and although they'd been together for several months, that sight usually took his breath away. But not this evening. What he had experienced that afternoon squashed his desire, making him forget what he and Kate had planned. She had not. The top button on her blouse was already undone.

"You're not going to believe it!" he blurted out.

Kate had a mental flash: *Art had learned something about his birth parents.* She didn't share this or any other insight with him because she was nervous her extrasensory perception would scare him away. Like it had with other boys, who got spooked when they discovered she knew all they thought about was having sex. "What happened?" she asked.

"It scared me. It was so real and freaking unbelievable at the same time!"

# CHAPTER 3

A YEAR AGO, AFTER HER MOTHER, LENA, died from a horrific fall from a horse, Kate's Aunt Peg reluctantly agreed to let her niece live with her. After she heard Art's amazing story, Kate went to the building where her aunt's apartment was and climbed to the fifth-floor, pausing outside her aunt's door. She listened for the ranting all-news channel her aunt always had on high volume. Quiet. Phew! Angry Ant, as her friend Rita had nicknamed Peg, was out, most likely at the local bar where she drank shots of cheap bourbon with beer chasers. Alone.

Kate entered the apartment, went into her closet-sized bedroom and closed the door. Then, she squirmed out the window to the fire escape and walked down one flight to knock on a window. Rita's head popped out.

"Can you go up?" Kate asked.

"Up" was the roof, their private sanctuary for wishes and dreams.

"What's happened? You the first summer intern at your Columbia lab to be offered a full professorship?" Rita laughed.

"Equally implausible."

"Implausible? Dumb it down, AP Girl."

"Art just told me something really weird."

"Oooh, I can't wait."

The girls had met on the fire escape where Kate had sought refuge from anger TV. One autumn night reading by flashlight, she met Rita, who was avoiding her parents' nightly duel of insults. She invited Kate to the roof, where technically, no tenants were allowed. But EMT-trainee Rita had helped the building maintenance man clean and bandage a gash on his daughter's arm. So he looked the other way when the girls went up there to share their dreams or talk about the new hot guy Rita had just met.

Tonight they talked as they leaned against the parapet wall, looking out over the roofs of the neighborhood buildings. Angry Ant called them the odd couple—Kate was long and lean, and her best friend was short and a little squat. Rita took a hit from a joint, nodding to the darkening clouds shimmering in the light of a half-moon. "When the sky's like this in the movies, you know some shit's going to happen." She offered the joint to Kate, who declined.

"So, let me get this straight," Rita said. "The old crank with the waist-length beard claims to be a wizard, and he tells Art, the homeless dishwasher Art, that he's the rightful king of England? Oh, but not today or tomorrow—1,200 years ago, and to get there, Art'll travel back through time with them. But wait," she mimicked a TV pitchman, "there's more. Young teen king will lead an army to overthrow a sorceress bitch who illegally declared herself queen in his absence, thus heroically ending a civil war destroying the country."

"Sounds like some wacko version of the *King Arthur and his Knights of the Round Table* story, doesn't it?"

"I love those movies where sweaty, hunky guys beat each with swords. But what do they want from Art?"

"Nut cases trying to recruit him into a cult maybe?"

"He didn't buy into any of their bullshit, did he?"

"Well … you know how obsessive he is about discovering who and where his birth parents are."

"Yeah. My cousin adopted a child from Chile, and the kid moved there to try to find his real mama and papa."

"These guys somehow knew about Art's fixation and told him heroic stories about a king called Uther who was his real father."

"1,200 years ago?"

"Yup."

Rita took a toke. "If I'd been kicked around as much as Art has, I might believe there's a better place where my 'rents welcome me home, even if it's in another country and a whole other century."

"Yeah, but why couldn't that be some normal place like Iowa?"

"Where's the romance in Iowa, whatever that is?"

Kate shook her head. "But the king thing isn't even the wildest part. Art said that when he challenged the so-called wizards' magical powers, the old guy pointed a finger and lifted Art off the ground about a foot!"

"You're shitting me?"

"He really believes he floated off the ground."

"Just so you know, the diagnosis in my EMT books for humans who think they levitate is 'cuckoo in the noggin.' So I don't care how good a kisser the love of your life is. You might have to settle for a timid, rational nerd from your science high school." Rita inhaled, held her breath, then blew out the smoke. "But what if the old dude's for real? I don't care about the floating above the sidewalk bit, but abracadabra me tall and thin and drop-dead gorgeous, Mr. Wizard Guy."

"Why not ask him to get you into medical school?"

"Boring. Save a life here. Save a life there. How about beyond-beautiful Rita does the time-travely thing to Olde England, where she takes sorcery lessons to stir up some serious mischief. Hop on the time train with me, girl. Art has the hots for you, so if he da king, you be da queen." Rita held up a finger. "Oh, and don't forget to bring Midol for the cramps."

The weed was making her friend a little silly, but Kate also trusted that streetwise Rita saw through boasts, bluffs, hollow explanations, and nuttiness. Kate had known Art for only a few months, and he could have odd or menacing personality secrets she hadn't discovered yet. *Does levelheaded Art take hallucinatory drugs? Is he maybe cuckoo in the noggin?*

*Delusional. It was what a shelter therapist* had called Art if he continued to think he could right every wrong in the world with his fists. That headshrinker had arranged to have Art evicted from a youth home in the Bronx to an uncared-for shelter in Harlem. Art was sure the head shrinkers at this new place would check the delusional box on their forms if he told them he was royalty.

His room was larger than the prison cell he once had to spend the night in, but not by much. At least he wasn't sleeping in a gym-sized room with a hundred other kids like the last shelter he was in. The additional bed in the room was empty for now. Too restless to sit, he stood at the metal bureau he used as a desk as he searched the internet on his phone.

He'd always been fascinated with warriors and loved playing with miniature lead figures representing King Arthur and his Knights of the Round Table. But after his foster father melted the toys into a metal puddle as retaliation for not crying when he was spanked, Art put the idea of kings and knights out of his mind. He remained entranced with the military, studying the lives of the great generals: Alexander, Napoleon, Grant, and Patton. But he knew next to nothing about English kings.

He discovered that there was no Arthur on the official list of English kings. There were, however, several historical and legendary figures who could have served as inspiration for the many stories about King Arthur. Some of these tales were similar to what the two guys at Nikos' Diner spun for him. Especially the one where baby Arthur was taken away from Camelot to protect him from sorceress Morgan Le Fay's murderous mother.

Art was deeply engrossed when a sharp rap on his door startled him. "Art Penn?" More a threat than a question. A too-thin man with graying hair combed over a bald spot barged in. "I'm Mr. Little, your caseworker."

Art expected no affection and only scraps of respect from adults. A lesson at an early age in his foster home. They gave him little support and less love, believing that Art's constant fighting was a mental disorder. Youth shelter counselors checked off the "belligerent troublemaker" box on their forms and routinely transferred him to other facilities. Despite all the mistreatment, Art still judged people by their actions and attitudes, and he extended his hand. "Nice to meet you, sir."

Mr. Little returned a perfunctory shake and opened a file folder he carried. "You're new to us, Penn," he said, checking a form box and scanning the bare walls. "No pictures?"

Art had stopped putting up photos of Kate because kids stole them for the frames or to do whatever while staring at the attractive girl with a radiant smile. "Haven't gotten around to it."

Mr. Little touched the medal on a ribbon hanging off a bureau handle. "New York State karate championship." He sounded accusatory. "So you can channel your aggression, if only in a tournament setting."

"I don't start fights, sir. The big kids pick on the little ones, and someone has to defend them."

"That's not what I read in the reports. You have to learn to control your anger, boy." He shut the folder. "Our facility is sanitary and safe. We have Ping-Pong and a library with over seventy books. The TV in the dining room is always on except at mealtimes." His monotonous voice made Art sleepy. "Past misconducts don't count against you.

Every new resident starts with a clean slate. But we are a zero-tolerance facility." He slapped a booklet into Art's hand. "One infraction of our rules, and you're out. Do I make myself clear?"

"Yes," Art muttered. Mr. Little had not earned a respectful "Yes, sir."

It confused Art that grownups believed liars who told them what they wanted to hear. But he had controlled his anger when Mr. Little automatically presumed Art wasn't telling the truth about how the fights happened. *Why doesn't he believe me?* Then Art realized he'd repeated the question Lancelot asked when Art doubted what he and the old guy had told him was true.

*A wizard and a knight? From another world? Another time? Aliens.*

Sometimes Art felt like that. Not the outer space kind. More like he was a stranger in New York from another country where the weak and the poor who were abused found justice.

So, had he time-traveled to the twenty-first century as an infant? Kate had ridiculed the idea of time travel as being scientifically impossible, and her skepticism when he told her about floating above the pavement made his stomach churn.

It boosted his self-esteem that brilliant Kate believed his strength was "emotional intelligence" and admired his infallible bullshit detector. Although she did worry he was fearless to the point of recklessness. There was one thing that scared him: that she would wake up one morning and realize, "I'm going to be an award-winning chemist creating miracle drugs or pollution-eating microbes. Art almost flunked out of high school. He didn't bother applying to college. What was I thinking by getting involved with a dishwasher?"

He shook his head to chase away the thoughts about this king and time-travel bullshit.

# CHAPTER 4

UNSUCCESSFUL IN PERSUADING Arthur that he was royalty, the wizard realized he and Lancelot would have to remain in the present longer than expected. They needed modern clothes, a place to stay, and money. SUV driver Geoffrey chauffeured them to a clothing store and helped them choose outfits. At the next stop, they bought what Geoffrey said were the most essential tools of the twenty-first century: cell phones. Then he brought them to a large hotel near Times Square and stopped at the entrance. A platinum blonde jaywalked in front of the SUV, and Geoffrey tapped the windshield. She turned, giving him her extended middle finger and a playful gap-toothed smile. Merlin leaned forward, eyes riveted, then sat back.

"Makes the sap rise, don't it, Gramps?" Geoffrey laughed.

"I thought she might be someone I once knew."

"She must have been something. Gap-toothed ladies are luss-tee."

The wizard and Lancelot got out. Merlin had already rumpled his new clothes enough to pass for a professor. In his tight-fitting shirt and pants, Lancelot was oblivious to the teenage girls and young women ogling him as they walked by. Geoffrey pulled a large leather duffel bag and shopping bags from the back. "You guys almost look native," Geoffrey said, then frowned, indicating Merlin's waist-length white beard. "Almost. If you need more expert local knowledge, or your time travel tickets expire, give me a shout." When he saw their blank expressions, he held up his cell phone. "Call me."

When Squire Lancelot traveled to Jerusalem on a crusade, he was delighted by the shrines, temples, and bustling markets. But what he saw here confused the hell out of him. Why were so many people in what looked to be the city's main square? The only crowds of this size he'd seen in Camelot gathered to witness beheadings. Was the king or the sheriff going to execute someone? Did the peasants who zipped along on two-wheeled platforms without apparent effort have magic?

His uneasy feeling didn't lessen inside the hotel. While Merlin talked to a man with weakness in his eyes at a waist-high wooden barrier, Lancelot ran his finger over a chair's golden armrest, then poked the plush red velvet seat cushion. Gold decorated the chair and the frame around a mirror that was twice as tall as a man. Hundreds of sparkling diamonds with sunlight inside dangled from the ceiling. No wealthy noble in ancient England could display these riches. Not even the king. *The people who own this palace do not live by the Code of Chivalry. They relish monetary reward, not shun it.*

The desk clerk handed Merlin two plastic cards and a thick stack of paper. "Here's the cash advance on your credit card, Mr. Merlin, and your room keys."

"Keys?" When Merlin stayed in a hotel seventeen years ago, doors had metal keys. "To—gain—entry—to—your—room," the clerk enunciated like he was talking to a three-year-old. "The porter will take your suitcases and shopping bags to your room. James!"

A slouching young man sauntered around the counter, lifted the duffel bag with one arm, and then dropped it. "Whaddya got in here? A body?"

"Of course not," said Lancelot. "'Tis my chain-mail armor and broadsword."

James didn't so much as grin. "A comedian."

He picked up the bag with two hands, dumped it on a luggage cart along with the shopping bags, and wheeled it to an elevator. "After you, gents," he said.

The elevator moved up, and Lancelot reached for the wall to steady himself. "Egads! The room ascendeth!"

"I guess you don't have moving rooms we call elevators back on the farm." James eyed the guests. "So … you just visiting or in town for a little business? Either way, you should catch a Broadway show or grab a forty-ounce T-Bone. But if all the musicals are sold out, and you can't get a reservation at a steak house, ya call Jimmy." He pointed to the name tag on his uniform. "I got friends that got tickets and reservations, with a little extra for me, natch."

"We hath no idle time for shows," Lancelot said. "We est on a quest."

"A quest. Gotcha. What are you guys questing? Tall and thin? Debutant? Trash-talking? Hot Latinas? Asian? Big bazoombas?"

"I don't understand," Merlin said.

"Chicks. Fräuleins. Girls."

"We hath no interest in maidens," Lancelot declared.

"Okay, no shows, no maidens. If guys are your thing, I got guys. The same selection as the maidens, only you won't need the bazoombas."

Merlin shook his head. *Do these moderns think of anything besides sex?*

The elevator door slid open, and Lancelot didn't move. "The floor's nice and solid out there, big guy," Jimmy said. Merlin nudged the knight into the hall, followed by Jimmy, who used his master key card to open a door. Rolling the cart in, he muscled the heavy bag onto a luggage stand with an exaggerated groan. Then, he just stood there. Merlin's "Thank you" was more a "Now you leave."

"We got a custom in the city. I provide you with a service, and you show gratitude by giving me a gratuity."

"The word has not entered the English language where I come from," Merlin said.

"Let me educate you. It's a tip, and that's moola, dough, green-backs, Jacksons."

Merlin offered a hundred-dollar bill from his stack of cash. Jimmy eyed the bill suspiciously, then grabbed it. "Thanks, pops!" And bounced out.

Merlin collapsed on one of the double beds and searched his pockets until he found his new cell phone. His face beamed with delight as he turned it on. "So much magic crammed into this little box!"

Lancelot looked around, wondering how something in the ceiling glowed like the sun. Then, in an adjoining room with white stone walls, he saw a white bowl half-filled with water that resembled the wooden commode in his father's castle. But what was that silver thing? He wiggled the handle, and the water disappeared. "Oh!"

The floor-to-ceiling windows in the bedroom overlooked Times Square, and in the eye-assaulting ads on the mammoth screens attached to surrounding buildings, the women appeared twenty-feet tall. "Merlin, giant maidens!"

But the wizard was engrossed in his phone, watching a video of the Earth taken from a satellite. Eventually he said, "Tomorrow, we shall find Arthur, and if he still can't acknowledge his rightful place, I will use my powers to persuade him."

"And then we canst leave this godless time."

A bright light streaked across the sky above the tall buildings and was gone in a nanosecond. *So many things here I narry understand!*

A *hawk surrounded by a bright glow* rocketed through low clouds illuminated by the "city that never sleeps" and landed on the roof of a Midtown building. The bird morphed into a sinewy, high-cheek-boned teenager with flaming red hair cascading down her shoulders. Perching on a parapet nearby, a bored crow yawned, unimpressed by the transformation.

The teen dusted feathers off her full-length green gown, straightened her leopard-skin shawl so its claws faced outward, and adjusted the gold snake bracelet with ruby eyes coiled around her left forearm. Two pouches hung from a sash around her waist, and she checked to see if the gems, herbs, and roots inside were damaged. She tilted her head as if searching for the source of a distant sound or smell and sensed what she had come to find. *My spies alerted me that Merlin hath come to this place and time. But where?*

Morgan had no idea what to expect when traveling from seventh-century England to modern-time America. The surrounding skyscrapers that seemingly touched the clouds were much more magnificent than her castle and stirred envy in her. She went to the roof's edge and marveled at the shiny-wheeled vehicles magically moving without being pulled by horses or oxen.

Looking around, she spotted the crow. "Wherefore am I?"

For several years, the crow had been the pet of a poetess who taught it English by reading aloud articles from gossip magazines and fashion tips from *Vogue* and *Elle*. So the crow could understand humans—and it figured that the pretty young woman who entered the city on a lightning bolt, not a Greyhound bus, must be a sorceress who might understand crow-speak. "Well, you're not in Kansas anymore," the crow cawed.

"What est this Kansas?"

*Finally, a human with a bird brain.* "Kansas is farmland. You're in the Big Apple, city of big dreams and bigger disappointments."

"Crow, thou willst be my servant."

"I've got a blue bird's nest to rob and some roadkill on Eighth Avenue that looks promising. Have a nice visit." It flapped its wings and only got a few feet up when Morgan pointed her finger, forcing the crow to thud onto the rooftop. "Ugh! That wasn't very subtle."

"Subtlety est for thy poets, not the queen."

"Let me guess. You didn't read the Thirteenth Amendment with your morning coffee. Enforced servitude happens to be illegal, even in New York City."

"In year 773, every bird, beast, and human boweth to me. I est Morgan Le Fay, Queen of Camelot and all of England. I est the law and thou willst obeyeth my commands and address me as Your Majesty."

If it tried to fly away again, the self-important redhead would likely point that hurtful finger. *Maybe being a servant of a queen with magical powers could be droll.* Crow spread its wings, cocked its head to one side instead of bowing, and in rap-singer cadence said, "Yo Ma-jes-ty."

"I senseth that Arthur est not afar. He willst be with an old man who est addicted to venison pies. First, I findeth the pie maker where Merlin willst trade for his meals. You will follow Merlin, who willst lead you to Arthur. Take me to the pie maker, Crow."

"There are probably hundreds of venison pie makers in this city."

"Then this instant we shalt start."

"Don't take this as an insult, Your Dowdiness, but you're dressed like you stumbled out of a low-budget princess movie. As luck would have it, you landed on the city's most exclusive women's clothing store. Use your magic to open that entry, and we'll set you up with clothes made in this millennium." Crow nodded at the leopard-skin shawl and snake bracelet. "And accessories that are a little less biker-chick."

Morgan Le Fay pointed to the metal door, which exploded out of its frame, skimming just above her head.

"Yes!" The crow flapped its wings in appreciation. *This promises to be more than just amusing. Maybe there'll be an article about us, and I'll be the first crow to make the cover of New York Magazine!*

In the department store, the crow perched atop an eerily pale female mannequin in a dimly lit, vast designer clothing area. Morgan emerged from a dressing room wearing a bright yellow gown with a flowing skirt decorated with sequins.

"Now really, Your Royal Tastelessness. Take it from a recently enslaved but erudite servant. You don't want to walk around the streets of New York looking like you're going to an eighth-grade prom in 1953." Indicating the racks of dresses, "There's Dior. Calvin, Versace. Try on one of their classy sleeveless sundresses, and you'll like what you see. And those leather pouches of yours look like they belong on a lumberjack's belt. So we'll need a nice shoulder purse and shoes to match. And without mud or cow poop." Crow sniffed. "Or both."

*When she reached Aunt Peg's apartment,* Kate was disappointed to hear the angry TV. Peg was in there and most likely drinking. Kate silently opened the front door and tried to sneak into her bedroom, but Peg saw her. "I put a roof over your head and feed you, and how do you repay me? With ingratitude. You got your internship paycheck today." Aunt Peg rubbed her thumb and fingers together. "Gimme."

Kate took a folded check out of her jeans pocket. "I'm grateful." *But I really don't like you.*

Kate went into her room and used a stick to prop the door closed due to its broken latch. The space was too cramped for a chair, so she lay on the lumpy mattress. She promised herself she would move on as soon as possible. Her only surviving relative was her grandmother Agnes, and Kate would love to share an apartment with the wise, worldly woman who'd lived unbound by convention, but she was in her nineties and in a nursing home. So Kate had no other place to go. Almost in protest, she'd made no effort to turn the cramped bedroom into her personal space. There was a photo of her jumping a horse over a high fence. And another of herself with her bundled-up mother and grandmother on a wintery beach. All three of their smiles could have melted the snow.

Kate focused on the poster of pilot Amelia Earhart standing on top of a twin-engine L10 Lockheed Electra airplane, feet spread, hands on her hips, and eager for adventure. Amelia was the first woman to attempt to fly around the world almost one hundred years ago. But her life ended tragically when her plane disappeared over the Pacific Ocean. Sometimes Kate broke free from this depressing room in the cheerless apartment by imagining she was at the controls of that Electra. Until she met Art, she always flew solo. Now he was her copilot. A tap on the window jolted her out of her reverie.

"You flying away again?" It was Art. He often climbed the fire escape to avoid an unpleasant encounter with Angry Ant.

"We're cruising 20,000 feet above a vast and sparkling sea."

"Want to go for a run?"

Kate had raced in the mile event for The Bronx High School of Science girls' track team, and she loved how worrisome thoughts vanished with exertion and distance. Their usual route was the 6.2-mile loop inside Central Park, but today they explored Riverside Park near the Hudson River.

They both had trouble finding a comfortable stride—casting each other cautious, sideways glances. Was it because they'd discovered unknown things about each other with their separate reactions to the encounter with the old man and the young guy who said he was a knight? Art was wondering why Kate had been so strident in her dismissal of time travel. For the first time, she seemed unsettled by Art's apparent lack of education and naivety.

Simultaneously, they picked up the pace. Art's idea of endurance was exponentially more extreme than hers, but Kate was proud she could keep up. As they neared the end of their planned run, Kate started to sprint. She could beat him in short bursts, which she did today, although she questioned whether he let her win. Minds cleared and with exhilarated smiles, they bent over to catch their breaths.

To get back to the Upper East Side, they headed through Columbia University at 116th Street and Broadway. The university's logo of a shield with three crowns above the Latin motto: *In Lumine Tuo, videbimus lumen* decorated the ornate metal arch over the west entrance to the main campus. "Why the crowns?" Art asked.

"This is the oldest college in America, charted by King George II when New York was a colony, and its original name was King's College." Then she read the Latin and translated: In thy light shall we see light.

He shook his head. "How many languages do you know?"

"A couple."

More than that, he knew. But she'd never made him feel inadequate that he could only speak one.

The main quadrangle was mostly deserted since the summer semester had ended, and the fall semester had not yet begun. Being among the majestic libraries and imposing academic buildings put a bounce in Kate's step. She pointed to a red brick building. "That's Chandler, where I'll take most of my chemistry classes."

The campus had the opposite effect on Art. Feeling dumb in almost any classroom, he knew he would be trapped and claustrophobic in these buildings. "You know that birthmark on my left foot?" he asked.

"Yeah, what made you think of that?"

"Seeing the crowns got me thinking of kings and those guys. They knew about the birthmark."

"Maybe they had a computer at their asylum and found your medical records online."

He had to show her he hadn't been committed in the same institution. "Hey, where do teenagers learn to fight dragons?"

"Hollywood?"

"Knight school."

They both groaned. But that he could tell a dumb joke eased her worries about his mental state.

Entering the north end of Central Park, they jogged up the Great Hill, not far from their private spot. At the top was a field surrounded by a cinder track where the city seemed far away. On this hot, sunny day, families picnicked, kids played bad soccer, and young women and men sunbathed in skimpy bathing suits. A solo saxophone player improvised "What a Wonderful World." It was Kate's favorite haven from the surrounding concrete and steel.

She and Art lay on the grass, tracing the outlines of the billowing clouds as an artistic summer breeze kept refining their shapes. After her mother died and her grandmother entered the nursing home, Kate had felt alone in this city of eight million people. Her few attempts to break through Aunt Peg's alcohol-fueled resentment were unsuccessful. Befriending Rita took the edge off the loneliness. Since she met and fell in love with Art, she no longer felt she was a single atom spinning in a solitary orbit. Reaching out to hold his hand, she realized that hot, soapy water had made his skin rough and chapped, and she wished she had lotion to soothe it.

Art rolled onto his side, leaning close to whisper. "I had a dream last night."

"A happy one?"

"Not happy or sad." He thought for a moment. "I have it over and over. A man leads an army into battle against enemy soldiers whose faces are covered in red horror masks. The man moves forward to fight, but that's when I wake up."

"Mom once told me that we're the heroes of our dreams. That would make you the boss or general or whatever."

He lifted the hand she held. "I wash dishes. High school was a struggle. I've got no family, no money." He took a deep breath. "But even when my back's aching at the sink, I know someday I'll face a life-changing challenge. I have no idea what it is, but I'm sure I'll have to fight to succeed. General Grant failed in civilian life, but he discovered his true strength and genius fighting for the cause of reuniting the country shattered by civil war."

"You showed me pictures of when you were a skinny kid, and you lifted weights until your muscles became ..." Kate caressed his bicep and cooed, "... silky steel. So I know you'll be victorious in whatever battle you must fight. And you're also empathetic and always treat me with the utmost tenderness. Maybe you'll be the general who ends wars."

"You think?"

"I'm positive."

He wished he had her certainty.

*Morgan Le Fay and Crow visited* six bakeries that made venison pies without finding any clues about a customer with a waist-long white beard. Crow was delighted to be the interpreter of the modern world for this sorceress, who loved the hustle and bustle of the city that matched her own energetic pace. Morgan allowed herself to be distracted from the hunt by the window displays in the clothing and shoe stores, particularly those shops on Madison Avenue.

What she didn't like in the city was all the walking, especially wearing the high heels she now favored. Crow suggested she rest her tired feet in the Palace Suite at a five-star hotel. It had enough gold and gilt to satisfy the queen's need for royal accessories. Surrounded by boxes of new shoes, Morgan put her legs up on a satin-covered sofa.

The sorceress had followed Crow's advice to lose the "eths" and "doths" if she wanted to blend into modern times. Morgan had perfect pitch and adapted her language to current American usage in a very short time. She'd also followed Crow's fashion advice about a sleeveless sundress. The low V-neck was her choice.

"You're looking foxy," Crow flattered.

"I have no resemblance to those rodent-eating vermin."

"You might not use that metaphor in the seventh century. It means that men will stop and look twice as you sashay along."

Morgan smiled. "I like this *foxy*." She thought for a moment. "Men are foxy fools."

She stood and studied her reflection in a full-length mirror. "Tell me, Crow, I see much loveless commerce in the land, but I must find a romantic place."

"Well, maybe the Bow Bridge in Central Park, where humans take wedding photos. But there's a body of opinion that weddings and romance don't go together."

"We shall go to this place, and Merlin will come tonight."

"How do you know this, Your Slyness?"

"My mother told me that when Merlin decided to hide Arthur in the future, a young nurse named Clarissa accompanied him to care for the infant, and the horny magician was smitten. But the gap-toothed beauty devastated Merlin by not returning to Camelot with him. I'll create a desire in his dreams that he cannot resist. And then, Crow, you will follow Merlin to Arthur."

"This Arthur must be hot."

"Like when I burn a traitor alive at the stake?"

"Not roasted, Your Royal Cruel-ness. Lusty, physically desirable."

"My only lust for Arthur is that he be roasted."

# CHAPTER 5

A WOMAN, HER PALE SKIN luminescent in the moonlight, beckoned. "*Merlin. I await you on the Bow Bridge.*"

The wizard jolted awake in his hotel room, absolutely certain the woman in his dream was Clarissa. Did she really wait for him at this place in New York City now? Of course it was improbable, but he couldn't miss an opportunity to discover if his long-lost love was real or just a dream.

He dressed silently so as not to wake Lancelot, then checked himself in the mirror, brushing a strand of white hair over a bald spot. *Old but dignified.* One corner of the room was cluttered with gadgets that Merlin thought demonstrated modern-day magic: video watches, ballpoint pens, paper not made of animal hides, comfortable running shoes, science books, aspirin, an electric toothbrush still in its package, several drones, eyeglasses. And electrified scooters for him and Lancelot. The wizard grabbed one and headed out.

At this late hour, only a few drunken revelers stumbled along the streets. Thick-shouldered men in work clothes with reflective strips hefted black bags into garbage trucks' roaring dragon mouths. Following directions on his phone, Merlin zipped through the empty streets on his scooter, his beard flowing behind him.

Central Park was surprisingly peaceful at three in the morning. Merlin cruised through soft circles of light cast by the streetlamps on the footpath beside the Boat Pond. There! Ahead, on the graceful arch of the Bow Bridge, a beautiful woman wearing a white diaphanous gown beamed a gap-toothed smile. But as he got close, she vaporized, the mist disappearing in a gust of wind. Lingering in the air was the sweet, sulfurous odor of the plant silphium that always emanated from the sorceress Morgan Le Fay. Merlin cursed that he'd allowed himself to be tricked so easily.

He knew her well. Born to the same father a year before Arthur, Morgan was not an heir to the throne due to King Uther's extramarital affair with a sorceress. As a young teen, she had apprenticed with Merlin to develop her natural magical abilities. But she resisted the moral restraints he placed on these powers and joined the coven of witches on the Isle of Orkney. There, she learned to increase her magical strength to equal Merlin's, but with no ethical restrictions. Good and evil became mere concepts for her.

In Camelot, Morgan was winning the war against the nobles who refused to recognize her as the rightful queen. But she knew the real threat to her sustained rule was Arthur. Merlin realized that to prevent her rival from time-traveling back to England to take the throne, Morgan had come to the present to kill him.

Merlin and Lancelot not only had to convince the young dishwasher that he was the king, they had to protect him from a homicidal sorceress.

*Arthur's mortal enemy's presence* in the city energized Lancelot. He would use his skills at arms, almost superhuman strength, and even his life to protect his king. The knight felt like he'd become a knight again. But in the hotel room, Merlin disguised Sir Lancelot as a hip-hop teenager.

"You doth humiliate my title," Lancelot protested, tugging at his underwear above his low-slung jeans, then pushing the sweatshirt hood off his head.

"Morgan will spot you immediately if you don't disguise yourself. Otherwise, you cannot fulfill your duty."

Lancelot swished his sword back and forth, then watched Merlin shape-change into an identical replica of Lancelot in more dignified clothes.

"Why art thou me?" Lancelot asked.

"I will lead Morgan's spying crow in the wrong direction. Wait for two hours." He handed Lancelot a digital watch. "It's how they mark time here. Then go out the hotel's back entrance, take the subway to prevent Morgan's bird spies from following you, collect Arthur, and bring him to The Cloisters. It's a replica of a medieval monastery not far from the diner, and he'll be safe in the chapel there. Morgan's sorcery doesn't work in sacred spaces." Then he added, "And leave your weapon here. The local sheriffs have outlawed broadswords. Even for knights."

"That explaineth the chaos on these streets."

*Morgan tried on a pair* of colorful high heels in a shoe store from which she could see the entrance to Merlin's hotel. Most of the customers overhugged little white dogs, but not Morgan. Her pet crow perched on the back of a loveseat.

"You sure this is the hotel you followed the old man to?" Morgan whispered, not wanting to alarm anyone by talking to a bird.

"Does Your Doubtfulness think I'm a birdbrain? Yes, I'm sure," Crow whispered, then nodded at the shoes. "Nice jimmies."

Merlin-Lancelot came out of the hotel, looked around, and spotted a white-necked raven that appeared to be focused on him.

In the shoe store, Morgan Le Fay said, "That guy might look like Lancelot, but he's stoop-shouldered—it's Merlin, who shape-changed into the knight. Do you have a bird following him, Crow?"

*Nag nag.* "As commanded."

Merlin-Lancelot got into a cab, which whisked him away from the hotel. High above, the raven followed.

When impatient Lancelot couldn't find the rear exit, he disregarded the wizard's instructions and went out the hotel's front door. Morgan immediately spotted the teenager whose bearing contradicted his hip-hop attire. The real Lancelot! Carrying his scooter, he descended into the subway station. When the train wasn't there, the knight climbed the exit stairs three at a time to zoom away on his scooter—disregarding Merlin's instructions once again.

Morgan had correctly anticipated that the knight's impetuousness would eventually put her victim at risk. "He'll lead you to Arthur, Crow. Follow him."

# CHAPTER 6

ART CHANGED OUT OF his soiled work shirt in the diner bathroom. He was slump-shoulder tired after his ten-hour shift, but the thought that he was about to be with Kate brightened his spirits. As he headed out, Nikos beckoned to him to sit in a booth, and it unnerved Art that his boss had on his serious face.

*Crow flew high above the hip-hop knight,* who scooted rapidly along the sidewalk and stopped outside Nikos' Diner. The bird swooped down to the front window, where he saw a young man with one blue eye and one green eye sitting in a booth. *Here is the man the queen desires.* It flew away to report the good news.

*Nikos leaned toward Art.* "You work hard as a donkey. You come on time. You never complain. The cooks can't figure out why a strong, good-looking, smart guy like you is washing dishes. Me also. So, no more work for you."

"What?" Art was shocked. "What did I do wrong?"

"You run without arriving, son. Find good work where you use your muscles and mind to protect people."

Art's jaw muscles clenched. "But I need this job."

Nikos handed Art an envelope with a thick wad of bills inside. "There must be a thousand dollars here!" the astonished dishwasher said.

"It'll give you time to discover the right thing."

No one had ever treated him with such kindness and encouragement. "I'm really grateful, Nikos. But I can't take your money."

"It ain't no gift. It's a loan, and the vig's double-digit."

Art knew when this mild-mannered guy used a gangster term for loan interest, he was kidding.

"Someday," Nikos continued, "you'll be eating ripe figs in a mansion by the Aegean, and I'll come to collect. Move in maybe, yes?"

To refuse Niko's generosity would be disrespectful. Art grinned. "How about this, I'll buy you that Greek island where you grew up so you can return to be king."

"Sounds like a plan. Now take the road before I give you the job again."

Art wasn't sure, but he thought he saw a tear in Nikos' eye. Now he had something else weird to tell Kate. *I got fired so I could have the opportunity to improve myself.* He bounded out of the diner and was annoyed to find Lancelot standing there.

"Will you please stop harassing me?" Art said.

"The sorceress wishes to slay thou. I will be at your side to protect my king."

"Sorceress?"

"A witch with destructive powers."

Art looked around. "I don't see anyone on a broomstick."

Suddenly, a car veered off Broadway. Lancelot lunged, knocking Art down to the sidewalk just as the vehicle hurtled by them and crashed into a storefront.

The knight jumped up. There were dangers in this world his senses were not alert to, that he could not anticipate. How could he successfully protect his king? Art stood and realized his hands were shaking. "I didn't see that coming. Thanks."

Art saw the car's airbag had deployed and the driver's door had popped open. The elderly driver was coughing from the residue of the exploding bag and shaking his head in puzzlement. "I don't know what happened. The accelerator stuck or something. I hit the brakes, but it was like a demon possessed the car."

Across the street from the accident, Crow landed on the shoulder of a scruffy woman pushing a shopping cart filled with empty cans and bottles. She may have been wearing rags, but her colorful high heels were out-of-the-box new. "Drat!" she said in Morgan's voice.

"Tell me, Your Royal Highness, to whom all humans and beasts of the field bow, why do you need to kill a lowly diner employee?"

"If he survives, he'll replace me as ruler of Camelot. So, my half-brother must die."

Crow nodded its head appreciatively. *This is getting positively biblical.*

*The police officers who responded* to the accident finished their report, and Art headed toward the subway. Lancelot scooted up next to him.

"Go away. You're bad luck."

"I saved thou."

"I wouldn't have been standing still on the sidewalk if you hadn't been blabbing shit about a sorceress."

Art strode away, walking under a wooden shed protecting pedestrians from debris that might fall off the building being constructed above. The heavy planking ended at the worksite entrance, where a truck spewed liquid concrete into a bucket the size of a small car.

The knight hurried to catch up. "I speaketh the truth. Morgan Le Fay hath time-traveled here from Camelot to kill you!"

Art didn't anger easily, but now he turned to confront Lancelot, ready to fight the bigger teen. "I'm serious," he said in a menacing voice. "Stop bothering me with your fairy tales!"

High above, Morgan had shape-changed into herself. She was sitting in a glass-enclosed booth atop a tall construction crane. She wore a hard hat, vest, safety goggles, construction pants—and glittering high heels. No clunky steel-toed work boots for her. Her hand with brightly colored fingernails maneuvered a control joystick to hoist the concrete-filled bucket until it reached a sufficiently lethal height. Morgan thought men's toys in the modern time, like this crane, were much more satisfying than playing with swords and lances. She pressed a button on the joystick, releasing the bucket from the cable with a loud snap.

Art reacted to the sound and instantly pushed Lancelot out of harm's way. The bucket smashed into the ground, missing them by inches, and showering the area and workers with semi-liquid concrete.

Lancelot wiped the muck off his face. Now he understood. Morgan was using her magic to cause these attacks. The battle had begun, and he was eager for this challenge, his adrenaline racing. Instinctively reaching for his sword, the knight felt an unfamiliar sense of vulnerability without it. "Doest thou now believe thy life is in peril this day?"

Art's heart was thumping wildly. He'd almost been killed by accidents twice in the last half hour. What was the probability of that? Something could be happening that he didn't or couldn't understand. "So what if I do think someone is trying to kill me?"

"I shalt take thee to a safe place where Merlin willst explain," Lancelot assured him.

Living on the street and in shelters, Art had heard his share of promises: from religious cultists offering him an escape from the anxiety and degradation of homelessness to gang members guaranteeing folding money and girls. He'd learned to doubt these and other seductions. His wariness radar wasn't detecting bullshit blips from this odd-speaking stranger spouting fairy tales. Maybe Long-Beard would have some answers.

*In the crane cab*, Crow offered, "Maybe you missed because you're still a little time-travel-lagged."

"The queen's aim is perfect," Morgan said. She pulled a makeup mirror from a pocket on her construction pants to check her hair color. It was faded barn-red, a sign that her powers had diminished. *But a sorceress with fading magic could miss. Time for a pick-me-up potion!*

*Lancelot was pleasantly surprised* by The Cloisters Art Museum set in a park at the north end of Manhattan. The stone buildings and court-yards, or cloisters, were replicas of medieval and Renaissance structures and didn't unsettle the knight like the alien buildings constructed of mirrors and steel. He was relieved to find a chapel similar to one he'd visited in France. Here, the sorceress could not harm Arthur. Nor him. He was grateful to discover a sacred place to thank God for safely delivering the king and himself from death. Lancelot knelt to pray before a small altar with its elaborately carved cross.

Having no religious beliefs, Art left the chapel to explore a gallery with decorative tapestries covering the walls. Were there really unicorns back then? Probably not. In a battle scene, mounted knights attacked foot soldiers, and Art guessed it wasn't going well for the men on the ground. One of the knights in the tapestry morphed into Merlin and emerged from the fabric.

Like the out-of-control car and the falling cement bucket, this was another thing Art couldn't explain. "How did you ...? How did you know what happened to Lancelot and me?"

"I can read your mind," Merlin said matter-of-factly.

*Read my mind?*

Arthur, do you ever wonder if there are forces in the universe that even the most modern and sophisticated science cannot explain?"

"Like transforming yourself from a woven image of a knight into a human?"

"If that is not magic, then what is?"

"I was hoping you'd have a rational explanation."

"Those attempts on your life cannot be explained by your reason, but you can understand why they occurred."

"I'm not sure that makes sense."

"Jealousy, the desire for parental approval, and anger at inheritance denied have caused royal villainy and murder throughout history. You're the legitimate heir to the throne in Camelot and Morgan Le Fay's only rival for the crown. So she needs to eliminate you. Easy to understand. What is inexplicable to you is that, like me, Morgan can travel through time, shape-change, throw dreams, and cast spells, as she did on a cement bucket and an automobile."

Art had never faced a situation where he could not find some logical explanation for its existence or motivation. But a time-traveling murderous half-sister? Truly beyond rational understanding.

"There you go with that crap again." He strode toward an exit, half expecting Merlin to do the finger-pointing trick again. But the wizard had a plan.

Lancelot finished praying only to see the young man whom he was honor-bound to protect striding out into the dangerous world.

"Guard him to his residence," Merlin directed the knight. "Then keep alert for the sorceress and her crow. Arthur will not be safe until Excalibur is in his grasp." The wizard touched the blue sapphire hanging around his neck. "I doubt we will ever convince the king that he is king. I'll arrange it so that he has no choice but to return with us."

# CHAPTER 7

THE ONLY OBJECTS NOT GOLD or gilded in her ostentatious hotel suite were an electrical hot plate and a black iron mini cauldron Morgan had set up on an antique writing desk. She added foul-looking ingredients from her leather pouch while enjoying a TV drama about treachery and avarice between generations in a modern-day family-owned business.

Morgan inserted her finger into the boiling liquid, then licked it. Staring intently into a mirror, the sorceress watched her hair intensify in color until it was almost neon red. Her magical powers were restored.

She rode in the limousine she had hired to the Morningside Youth Shelter, where Crow had followed Arthur and Lancelot from The Cloisters.

Art *now had a roommate,* a boy his age with a shaved head and skull and crossbones covering one arm. He obviously hadn't showered for weeks because his body odor polluted the room. To get some fresh air, Art struggled to open the window that had been painted shut. Below, he spotted Lancelot pacing back and forth across the street. *The guy's nuts!*

He heard "It's all I have in the world" from a young voice that had not deepened. He went to the open door to a room across the hall where a skinny teenager with a ponytail was scattering clothes and personal items from a suitcase.

A much younger boy curled up on his bed sobbing.

"Put the kid's stuff back in the suitcase," Art said evenly.

Ponytail spun around and grinned, holding out the palms of his hands to indicate he got the message to stop. "Okay. Okay. No harm done." Suddenly, he dove forward, trying to wrap his arms around Art. But the trained karate fighter nimbly stepped aside.

Other kids gathered in the hallway to watch and yelled enthusiastically, "Fight! Fight!"

Art has lost count of the number of fights he had been in where only one boy would be standing at the end, and from the evil in Ponytail's bloodshot eyes, this would be one of those battles. But his opponent's jabs and punches had no sting, more like they were to create the illusion of a struggle.

"Make way!" The shelter counselor, Mr. Little, barged into the room. "Stop this instant!"

Art stepped back to disengage, dropping his hands to his side, but Ponytail sucker punched him hard in the chest, and this one wasn't for show. Instinctively, Art karate chopped the boy's neck. The blow knocked him backward, and on his way down, his head hit the corner of a metal bed frame. He lay very still on the floor.

"Get back to your beds!" Mr. Little ordered, then pointed a finger at Art. "Stay right there!" The counselor knelt and felt Ponytail's neck for a pulse. "Oh my god, you've killed the new boy!"

*Crow perched on a windowsill* with a view of the room where the body lay on the bedroom floor, surrounded by detectives in suits and crime scene technicians in white coveralls. The bird fluttered down to the limo. "Your enemy just killed a kid, so he'll go to jail and won't be a worry for a long time."

Just then, two officers escorted Arthur out of the shelter. His hands were cuffed behind his back, but he held his head high and squared his shoulders. Morgan unsheathed a foot-long dagger and reached for the car door handle.

"Whoa, what up, Your Royal Impetuousness?"

"I'm going to kill Arthur."

"Those police will most likely shoot you if you do that." Crow pointed a bent leg at her. "Bang, bang. And that's a big ouch."

"They are just mortals, so I'll put a spell on them."

Crow swung its beak around to indicate the numerous uniformed and plainclothes police officers that populated the murder scene. "Not that I doubt your powers, but immobilizing all those dudes would take a lot of spelling."

"I'm the tainted fruit of adultery, the bastard daughter scorned by my father, the king. I'm banished from the castle, denied any claim on becoming queen. Oh, but Arthur. He's the favored first son. He inherits the throne. I learned Latin and French and studied sorcery, an excellent skill in controlling one's enemies, while he knows how to scrub pots and pans. So understand Crow, I have to kill him myself. It's the only way to liberate my mind and heart from the distemper he causes."

The officers put Arthur in the back of a police car and sped away.

"Merlin wasn't nearby to protect Arthur, and he was still able to evade my dagger!" Morgan curses.

"I'm certain you'll devise a plot to find satisfaction."

But Morgan wasn't listening. She was so enraged, she squeezed the blade of her dagger until blood stained her designer sundress.

Crow shook its head. *Phew. Her Royal Neurotic-ness could use a session or two of family counseling.*

At the city morgue, two med techs in white protective suits rolled a stretcher with a black body bag into a room with floor-to-ceiling rows of large steel drawers. They opened one and pulled out a metal tray onto which they transferred the body bag. Then, pushing the tray back inside, they shut the door and left the room.

A few moments later, the handle on the drawer turned, the door swung open, and the tray rolled out. The zipper on the body bag unzipped, and Ponytail bolted upright, very much alive. "Phew. Body bag ventilation is worse than the last time I was in a cow's stomach," he muttered. Then, he shape-changed into Merlin.

The wizard ran his hand over a steel table with gutters running along the edges. He was fascinated by the tool with a sharp circular blade hung underneath. When he touched a button, the blade rotated rapidly. *For cutting? What is this place?* He opened a large drawer and pulled out a tray with a thoroughly dissected human male. The chest cavity was open, revealing all the internal organs. The top of the skull was neatly cut off, and Merlin understood what the circular saw was for. The wizard had visited battlefields to study bodies and heads that had been slashed open, but never had he seen human anatomy revealed with such order and completeness. He could find the answers here to many questions about the human body if only he had time to study this corpse. Alas, he did not.

By getting himself "killed" by Arthur, Merlin set in motion events that would cause unendurable distress and disruption for the young king in the modern world. And the wizard knew his mission had hardly begun.

*That same night, Art felt* the lifeless eyes of the Ponytail kid tracking him as he paced back and forth in the cramped jail cell. The stink of disinfectant couldn't mask the odor of anxious piss. Art's stomach rumbled, yet he had no appetite. The baloney sandwich on stale bread went uneaten. He looked at his fists that had broken noses and opened cuts above bullies' eyes. He'd injured but never killed. He wished he'd encountered the bully in a way that didn't lead to a fight. Until now, he had never regretted his choices or second-guessed his decisions. But now, crushing remorse filled him with doubt about what kind of person he was.

In momentary flashes, Art envisioned Ponytail twisting his body like he'd *intentionally* aimed the back of his head at the metal bed frame. But there was no way he could do that, right? *Is my brain trying to give me an excuse so I'm not a killer?*

He'd been dumped into the challenged-kid classes, suspended from high school for fighting, and kicked out of his foster parents' house. Homeless, he slept under a bridge with a knife in his hand. No one would hire him except for gruff-talking, soft-hearted Nikos. Yet, after each setback, Art had the determination to get back up and keep going. But murder?

He might be knocked down permanently this time. Would the cash Nikos gave him be enough to hire a lawyer to keep him out of prison? Probably not. So he'd be convicted. Then, prison—where he'd have plenty of unwanted opportunities to fight hard boys.

And he worried about Kate. They saw each other or talked every day. She'd be concerned when he didn't answer his cell. As soon as they let him make a call, he'd let her know what happened. But how would full-scholarship Kate, beautiful Kate, charming without groveling Kate, react? What would go through her mind when she discovered what he'd done? *Hi, this is my boyfriend, Art. Don't mess with him. He killed a boy with his bare hands.*

The image of the girl with a red bandanna around her blond hair popped into his head, and he became momentarily distracted by the memory of the day they'd met in early spring. He'd taken the train north up the Hudson Valley to hike on the rocky hills next to the river. His shoelace broke, and he was sitting next to the trail knotting the pieces together when he looked up to see a girl who could've been the radiant and beautiful Princess Diana's twin. She pulled new laces still in their package from her backpack. "Will these help?"

This was Kate—of course she had extra laces in her pack. Later, he would understand that "just-in-case Kate" had something in her backpack for any contingency: a multi-tool Swiss Army knife, folding corkscrew, a granola bar to share with a less thoroughly prepared friend.

They started climbing together on the cool fall day, and soon, Kate challenged Art by increasing the pace. They raced to the top, bumping into each like puppies, laughing at nothing like old friends. Art had been to this summit many times to gaze over the cluster of gray buildings across the wide river: the United States Military Academy, West Point.

"You a cadet there?" Kate asked.

"No," he replied. The Military Academy might be close geographically, and as much as he would like to enroll, admission was galaxies beyond his academic achievements, or lack thereof.

While on the trail, they were close to being physical equals, but their circumstances were not. Kate was already in the Columbia Honors Science program for brilliant high school seniors. In the fall, she'd enter the freshman class there. Art barely had good enough grades to graduate from high school, and he washed dishes for a living. He was immediately captivated by this girl who seemed so nonjudgmental. She was attracted to this boy/man with no defenses. They had what Kate called "good molecular chemistry" that "dissolved" their differences. It was night by the time they took the train back to the city, and he remembered they held hands walking along. What was it she said at her building? He distinctly remembered she wanted to ask him up to the apartment but couldn't. Something about a mean aunt. He made a joke about his place not being so private either, which disappointed him after she kissed him goodnight with the same eagerness he felt.

*Do not obsess on that here!* No place to take a cold shower to extinguish the heated memory. One hundred push-ups followed by one hundred sit-ups put out only a little of the fire. He repeated this sequence until exhaustion dulled his brain, and he thankfully fell asleep.

*Rita poked her head through* Kate's bedroom window. "He answer his phone yet? He text?"

Kate was sitting cross-legged on her bed, her laptop glowing in front of her, and she shook her head, no.

"Was it something you said?"

Her head shook again.

"Something you didn't say?"

Kate shrugged and indicated the screen on her laptop. "Those two loony guys told him his real name wasn't Penn, but Pendragon, the same last name as King Arthur in the myths. Pendragon. Mouth of the dragon."

Rita spread her arms theatrically. "I'm Rita Moreno. I have an okay voice and like to sing show tunes. Just one look in the mirror and I know I'm not the fabulous actress, singer, and long-legged dancer. I'm the other Rita Moreno, who's five foot two and lives in a walk-up apartment. So, his real name might be Arthur Pendragon, but he ain't no king."

"It's amazing how that whole King Arthur story still appeals to the modern world after thousands of years. Friendly old wizards. Honor-bound warriors who fight to protect rather than conquer."

"Boys will be boys, no matter how old." Rita swung her legs into the room and sat on Kate's bed. "Knights in shining armor saving damsels, fighting dragons. It's little boys playing king of the hill and bigger boys wagging their wee ... *weapons*. And don't get me started on magic. 'I'll be Cinderella—I'll marry the rich, handsome prince, only let's skip the part where I have to clean bathrooms.' Or, 'I'll be the first five-foot-two quarterback to be an All-Pro football player.' Give me a break. Magic is getting results without effort, training or intelligence."

"Stop planning to become a surgeon. You have the insight to become a psychiatrist."

"I'd rather cure people by cutting out the cuckoo part of their brains than trying to figure out why the gray matter has gone cuckoo in the first place."

Kate looked at her phone. "Do you think he joined a cult? Maybe those guys kidnapped him?"

"I dunno. Art's cute enough that if you two weren't playing Romeo and Juliet, I'd kidnap the snack and lock him in my bedroom until he pleads, 'No *más*.'"

"Sounds like an effective therapy, Dr. Moreno. I'll try that when I find him."

# CHAPTER 8

AS MERLIN AND LANCELOT RODE downtown in Geoffrey's SUV, the wizard didn't reveal that he'd shape-changed into a ponytailed bully who started a fight with Arthur, deliberately clunked his head on the bed frame, then quieted his heart until there was no discernible pulse.

Lancelot was convinced that the men in blue uniforms would erect a gallows in front of the homeless shelter and hang Arthur in the spot where he committed the murder. That was how they dealt with killers in Camelot. But Merlin assured Lancelot that this would not happen, except maybe in Texas.

Merlin needed Arthur to realize that being a murderer dashed any hope of achievement and self-realization in the present. To speed this along, the wizard disrupted the dishwasher's sleep with a nightmare.

*At a military recruiting storefront, Art, wearing civilian clothes, stands at attention in front of a poster-perfect marine in the full blue dress uniform. He hands over enlistment papers to a program where privates can attend college to become officers while on active duty. The square-jawed marine screams in a voice that sounds like he is shouting into an empty metal trash can, "No convicted killers!" As Art exits the storefront, the door becomes the entry to Kate's apartment building. She comes out smiling with her arm hooked into the arm of a tall, skinny science nerd, and they pass by Art as if he were invisible. As this door shuts, it becomes the entry to Nikos' Diner, and on it is a handwritten sign: "Killers not worthy to wash dish!!!"*

Art woke suddenly, sweating and agitated. His worst fears about his future had vividly haunted his dreams. He figured he was tough enough to take his lumps in prison. But after his release, no marines, no Kate? Not even the endless mind-numbing drudgery of kitchen work? Breathing heavily, he had an overwhelming feeling of hopelessness.

A mouse squirmed out of a thin crack between the cinderblocks in the cell wall. Art had seen plenty of mice in homeless shelters, so he didn't shy away, especially from this little guy sitting upright in front of him. "You're pretty dumb to break *into* prison, Mr. Mouse."

*Morgan carried a food tray* down a long corridor lined with cells. She wore a corrections officer's shapeless, functional uniform and designer high-top sneakers that would be regulation at a hip downtown nightclub, not a city jailhouse. Her soon-to-be victim had no place to hide, no wizard to protect him now.

Perched on her shoulder, Crow averted its head from the strawberry yogurt. The bird's hypersensitive sense of smell detected what no human could: a poison potion Morgan had cooked up in the hotel suite and disguised in the yogurt.

"Bye-bye, half-bro," Crow cawed.

*Art's brain could not compute* what his eyes had just witnessed. Was he hallucinating? The mouse had transformed into the old guy with the long beard named Merlin, who promised to take him back to Camelot, where he would be safe from prosecution for murder.

"Impossible!" Art said.

"You witnessed me emerge from the tapestry, and now you've seen me shape-change into a mouse. So, you can trust that my powers will carry us there," Merlin assured him.

*Oh, man. What if he really could do it?* "But will that mean I'd never see Kate again?"

"You just had a dream about your future after prison."

"How do you ...?" *Of course. He said he can read minds. So he'd know my dreams too.*"

Merlin sniffed the air. "Silphium," he muttered. "We have to go this instant. It's not safe."

There was an urgency in his voice that startled Art. "What's wrong?"

"Morgan Le Fay is near. She'll kill you."

This was all beyond reason, but Art nodded. Merlin shape-changed Art and himself into mice, and they squeezed through the crack in the cell wall just as Morgan appeared. Her face contorted with rage, she howled a bird screech that no human voice could imitate.

"Well done, your Royal-Raptor. Welcome to the Aves classification!" Crow cawed.

Morgan blew out a breath and shook her shoulders to calm herself. "Have you ever been in love, Crow?"

"With something other than myself?"

"I experienced love once. It made me weak and careless. My sentimental brother will want to see that girl. Go to where she lives. He'll show up there and then we'll finish this adventure."

*After they escaped the cell*, the mice scampered through the prison's foundation to another crack that led to the sidewalk outside, where Merlin morphed them back into humans.

*What just happened? Am I really me again?* Art held his hands out to count his fingers. He made a fist, then relaxed his hands. He squeezed his arms. He took a deep breath, and his lungs were working.

"We must leave here before the police discover your cell is empty at morning bed check," Merlin said, ushering Art into a waiting black SUV. The round-faced driver with a CATS baseball hat turned, grinning. "Almost as exciting as the movie *Escape from Alcatraz!*"

The teenager who said he was a knight sat soldier-tall next to the driver and stared straight ahead. As soon as the doors shut, the SUV accelerated away from the curb, tires screeching.

Art knew he'd been transformed into a rodent, then back into a human. It was totally impossible. But here he was sitting on leather seats, smelling an evergreen scent refresher dangling from the rearview mirror, and driving through the city. It had to be real, but ...

"You've experienced powers in the universe you have denied exist, yet that I can control," Merlin said. "Do you doubt I can also travel forward and backward in time with whomever I wish to accompany me?"

Art shook his head. "But a minute ago, I would have sworn you couldn't change me into a mouse. Can you really time-travel?"

"When the stars are right, positively."

"So you break me out of prison to kidnap me to take me to ... what's it called back then ... Camelot?"

"You have a long journey before that challenge."

"My journey isn't yours." Art tried to open the door, but it was locked.

Merlin peered at an image of a large mausoleum on his phone. "I've never been to Ulysses S. Grant's Tomb. Isn't that an important memorial?"

"You want to go sightseeing when every police officer in the city will be hunting me? Sign up for a tour. I'm not your guide."

Art stared out the window. No pedestrians and few cars on the streets. A hollow city. Just like the feeling in his stomach. There was no safe place for him out there. Maybe anywhere.

A police car with vibrating lights and siren whoop-whooping pulled up behind the SUV. Art looked back. *It's over before anything begins.* But the cops rocketed by and kept going.

The driver, Geoffrey, stopped at 122nd Street and Riverside Drive, where Merlin got out. Art didn't budge, so Merlin pointed his finger to make Art float out of the SUV onto the sidewalk. "I'm curious what inspires you about General Grant," Merlin said. "Come."

Arthur knew he was powerless to refuse, so he followed the wizard down a slight incline to the plaza that was deserted in the pre-dawn hour. They continued to Grant's mausoleum, a massive marble dome set on a square foundation of granite. The heavy metal doors were closed.

"Shall we go inside?" Merlin asked.

"I'm sure it's locked."

Merlin pointed his arm, locks clicked, and the door swung open. A circular observation walkway with a low marble wall surrounded the burial chamber below, where the general's and his wife's bronze caskets were displayed.

Earlier in the season, Nikos gave him a weekend off work so he could take a bus to Gettysburg, Pennsylvania, where Union and rebel Confederate forces had fought a brutal three-day battle in July 1863. Art felt a profound communion with the soldiers who struggled and died there as he wandered around the gently rolling battleground park and military cemetery. It was as if their courage and fear and fighting spirit survived their deaths and radiated out of the once blood-soaked soil. Grant's Tomb didn't ignite the same intense feelings, but he did sense the great man's spirit endured in the mausoleum.

"You come here often," Merlin said.

Art had stopped wondering how this guy knew so much about him. "Yes. Grant was a great general leading the Union army to defeat the rebel Confederates. He was instrumental in reuniting a divided nation."

"You admire him?"

"Absolutely. Grant led brilliantly yet with compassion and no self-aggrandizement."

Merlin had calculated that this orphaned dishwasher would identify with a soldier who failed in civilian life but found unrealized strength and genius in battle. Arthur's birth father had not been there to guide him, so the boy had selected his ideal for inspiration: Ulysses S. Grant.

"A similar civil war rages in ancient Camelot between the nobles and their armies who support Morgan Le Fay, and those who oppose the false queen. But the opposition is losing because the nobles quarrel about who will be king."

The wizard swept his arm in a semicircle. A ghostly three-dimensional image appeared in the empty space above the caskets.

Soldiers and knights wearing tunics with snake and scepter logos were ransacking a primitive peasant village. Burning thatched roofs. Restraining the villagers in chains. This image dissolved into an army sieging a castle. Then, a new image showed six men hanging by their necks from a thick tree limb. And knights were fighting a desperate battle with other knights who had the snake and scepter images attached to their lances.

"Is this happening in England?" Art asked. "In the past?"

The wizard lowered his arm, and the images vanished. "If I had not discovered that you are brave, single-minded, and selfless, or had the character to succeed, I would have left you at Nikos' Diner. You will become the general with the divine authority and power to depose Morgan and end the civil war."

The idea of being a king who just sat on a throne in fancy duds didn't appeal to Art. But a warrior king leading an army in a desperate battle against an evil enemy. Yes! That was the image that invaded his dreams night after night. The confusion about shape-changing mouse magic and doubts about time-travel talk disappeared as if blown away by a fresh breeze. What he must do became crystal clear!

Art straightened his shoulders and, after slamming a resolute fist into his other hand, spread his arms. "Take me where I must go."


*Art believed he would join* the ranks of the cowards if he didn't tell Kate in person what his mission had become. So he persuaded the wizard and Lancelot to have Geoffrey stop at Aunt Peg's.

Art got out of the SUV and leaped high enough off the sidewalk to catch the bottom rung of a fire escape ladder. He pulled himself hand over hand to get to a platform and climbed the metal steps four stories to Kate's bedroom window. She was sleeping restlessly, tossing and turning. He hesitated for a moment, then shook his head and rapped softly on the glass.


*In the SUV, Geoffrey was singing* a happy song from a Broadway musical. He had been broke and living in his vehicle when the old man with the beard tracked him down. Somehow, Merlin knew he was an accomplished cook and offered him a job. Okay, that required time travel, but that was just fine. No debt collectors harassing him in the seventh century. And with this odd circus of a knight and a king and beautiful Kate, he was happy again. Happy enough to sing upbeat Broadway show tunes as they waited for Arthur.

At *the base of Kate's building*, Merlin was surrounded by a flock of pigeons as he scanned the sky. He knew Morgan was on the hunt for Arthur, and she'd likely shape-changed into a bird herself, or sent a spy. He sent the birds up to protect Arthur from being discovered.

High above, Crow circled lower and lower until it saw Art and Kate sitting on the fire escape. It whirled around to alert Morgan, but found itself facing a solid blockade of pigeons. "Make way, you rats with wings! I have important crow business!"

The pigeons pecked the crow with their beaks and swiftly managed to herd it into a pigeon coop on the roof of a nearby tenement building, then bolted the door.

"Guys, maybe there was a little misunderstanding," Crow cawed. "I said, 'Pats with wings.' Patriots. Patriotic pigeons have magnificent wings. Help a fellow feathered friend out here."

The pigeons flew away, and Crow hissed, "Like I said, rats with wings."

As *Merlin returned to the front seat* of the SUV, Lancelot looked upward at the fire escape where Arthur was exposed to the sky. "We doth need to protect our king from the evil sorceress."

"I have neutralized her spy. For now," Merlin said and stroked his beard. "Have you ever been in love, Sir Knight?"

"Absolutely," Geoffrey jumped in. "Sally, the barista with a tat of a butterfly over her entire back. Let me tell you, coffee wasn't the only thing she could roast. I fell hard for her and what'd she do? She dumped me for a guy with a motorcycle who was missing two front teeth."

"And you, Lancelot?" the wizard asked.

"I loveth my parents and I loveth God. But, no, I hath not been *in* love."

"Well, Arthur is in love, and his smitten heart does not feel the threat of death."

*On the fire escape,* Kate grasped Art's hand with I'm-never-letting-you-go pressure as tears of relief rolled down her cheeks.

"You escaped! You escaped from jail?" Her voice cracked with tension.

"Kate, are there things you can't explain in chemistry?"

"Why are you talking about chemistry? Aren't the police chasing you? Aren't you in danger?"

"Things are happening to me. I'm trying to explain them to you. And me."

"Well, probably the most basic mystery in chemistry is about the origins of life when there was nothing but inorganic matter on the planet. How did inert chemicals evolve to generate self-replicating, complex animated life forms? But what's that got to do with you getting out of jail?"

"My escape can't be explained scientifically. I was locked in a cell when a mouse crawled through the wall and magically became a wizard. He turned me into a mouse, enabling me to squeeze my way out through a tiny crack."

Kate felt a spark of fear. *Did he really believe this happened?* "If you're trying to be funny, I'm not laughing."

"I'm as serious as I've ever been."

She hoped she could puncture his delusions if she talked about concrete stuff. She calmly said, "This is Kate. I'm right here. Right now. I believe in my heart you're no murderer. It was an accident. I don't know how you really escaped, but if you're certain you can't get a fair trial, we can run and keep running. I have some money. We can buy a car. Mom had friends on an island off Seattle where old hippies grow marijuana and hide from the police. We can start a farm and raise a family. I can't live without you. I won't live without you, Art."

"Arthur."

Her body tensed. "Arthur?"

"You think an admissions essay about what I've learned about life by becoming a murderer will get me into college? What you're describing, a life on the run, always looking over our shoulders, wondering if the waitress serving us at a roadside diner will recognize two outlaws and call the police. That's not who you are. You're already soaring. I'm nothing but a weight around your neck, pulling you back to Earth. Your future is in the future. My future is in the past."

She punched him hard in the chest. "You effing kidding me?"

"I'm sorry to say I'm not."

"So you fell for their bullshit! The dishwasher's really a king, and His Majesty's leaving the peasant wench behind for her own good?"

Arthur started to put his arm around her but stopped, fearing she might think he would stay.

"Look up the list of English kings. No Arthur. No Uther," Kate said, her eyes flashing. It's a story. A myth, you dumbass."

*She had never played the dumb card before.* "England had many separate kingdoms before Arthur," he said, barely controlling his anger. "He united the country. Maybe before they started recording who the king was."

Kate's body slumped. *They've stolen my Art.*

"I know forever-certain that I'll never love another woman with every cell in my body like I love you."

"That fake romantic crap is supposed to make me feel better?" Tears streamed down Kate's face. "You're an impostor. You're not the person I'm in love with," she growled, pushing him away. "Go and don't ever come back."

# CHAPTER 9

THE SORCERESS WAS SCHEMING what misery she could deliver to Arthur when Crow squeezed through an open window. "What a night!"

"Did Arthur go to the girl?"

"As you predicted. The cad kissed her off, then got into a car. Your humble servant dutifully began to follow, but a flock of pea-brained pigeons locked me in a coop. It took me until an hour ago to peck my way out."

The sorceress let out her unearthly screech, and Crow thought, *I'm roadkill.*

But Morgan just ran her fingers through her hair. "There won't be a celestial event when Merlin can time-travel Arthur back to England for three weeks. We'll find him before that."

She went to the window and pointed at a young woman sitting at a large desk in an office tower across from the hotel. "Is that woman the queen of that mansion, Crow?"

"Well, it's a corner office, so she's the boss of something. Armani suit. Expensive haircut. But queen of the whole office building? More like a princess. If she owned the tower, she'd have better accessories."

"So who is the most powerful and feared queen here?"

"Power comes with money. The queen with the most money in this city owns the most and the best real estate."

*Hmmmm,* Morgan thought, then focused on her target. "Arthur won't be able to stay away from his lover, or she'll go to him. Get back to the girl's building, Crow."

"You mean sit on a boring fire escape all day and night?"

"That is what I command."

"Nevermore."

"Beware of angering your queen."

"I'm quoting a poem. Just a literary witticism. Not to annoy but to amuse."

"You should entertain ME, not your eater-of-dead-flesh self."

"Most certainly, Your Royal Smartness." (A sharp ear might have heard, "smart-ass.")

"And, Crow, when you flatter, do it with sincerity."

"The absence of that trait is yet another flaw in my character."

*The SUV moved along* a commercial strip where the businesses were mainly auto parts supply shops, off-brand gas stations, and bars. Geoffrey pointed at two young women wearing short skirts and high heels heading toward a bar with bull horns over the door.

"I think I'm in love," Geoffrey announced, then stomped on the brakes to avoid crashing into the car stopped at a traffic light. "You don't mind if I go in there and bring the ladies to where we're going, do you?"

"We hath notable work to do," Lancelot said.

"Oh, man. You making me drive you to a monastery or what?" Geoffrey whined.

Merlin consulted his cell phone. "Next left at the diner."

"Phew, you guys gotta lighten up and have some fun," the driver said as he turned off the main road onto a narrow lane leading into rural countryside. Sleek horses grazed on emerald grass behind freshly painted white fences. As he drove, Geoffrey serenaded the animals with a song about betting on a horse named Paul Revere.

Lancelot nudged Arthur. "'Tis Godly land, sire."

Arthur sat up. Maybe rural New Jersey resembled ancient England, where Lancelot wasn't the alien he was in the jarring, noisy city. In any case, the knight's neck and shoulders seemed less knotted with tension.

The houses here were unlike any Arthur had seen, except on TV. These were huge mansions surrounded by mowed football-field-sized lawns. Merlin directed Geoffrey to drive into a gravel driveway that wound through fenced pastures and then over a low rise. They came to a large house with white pillars that reminded Arthur of the mansions of Southern slave owners he'd read about. There were no other homes or farms in sight.

Puzzled, Arthur said, "We're in New Jersey, right? I thought you were taking me back in time."

"Yes, but only when you can fight like a knight and think like a king," Merlin told him.

They passed stables and a five-car garage attached to the main building, finally stopping by the grand entrance. Geoffrey jumped out first and, prying his cell phone apart, tossed the SIM card into some shrubbery. "Bye-bye debt collectors, bye-bye," he sang.

So Lancelot and Merlin were going to coach him. Getting mentally and physically ready for a rigorous hike or a fight in a karate competition usually energized Arthur. But now he worried what Kate was doing at this exact moment. Brushing her golden hair? Dressing for her internship? Weeping? Kissing some non-dishwashing scientist? And his shoulders sagged with misery.

Recognizing that Arthur was preoccupied, Lancelot said, "Come, sire. Nothing doth focus thy wits like combat."

*Lancelot and Arthur practiced* sword fighting for two hours without pause on the lawn behind the mansion. Both wore heavily padded garments on their upper bodies and arms, and their helmets had clear plastic protective face coverings.

Over and over, Lancelot used his lightning-quick reflexes to flick the sword out of Arthur's hands. Each time he picked it up, Arthur recited one of Lancelot's lessons. This time, it was: "Weight balanced on both legs with sword held high." This was similar to how Arthur learned to use his body in karate. The knight thrust his weapon, and nimble Arthur dodged the attack. Then, he used a recently acquired technique to knock the sword out of Lancelot's hand, wounding the knight's pride. Lancelot used his enormous strength to knock Arthur to the ground. He jumped up, only to be bashed to the ground again. And again. Arthur lunged forward, slashing with vicious strokes, which the knight blocked effortlessly. "Fury seldom conquereth skill," Lancelot instructed.

Arthur did not relent until his arms were dead with fatigue, and he felt he couldn't defend himself with his sword held high. Lancelot put the tip of his blade on Arthur's neck. "A knight never surrendereth to exhaustion or pain. Fight your enemy until he surrenders to his exhaustion and pain and thus doth lose the will to fight. Or live. Harden your body and harden your mind."

The blade at his throat made it very clear to Arthur how well he learned to fight with a broadsword could make the difference between life and death on the battlefield. Lancelot sheathed his sword.

"I'm not quitting practice," Arthur said.

"A knight doth not battle only with a broadsword."

He led Arthur into the mansion, where medieval weapons Merlin had purchased online were laid out on tables. "Select a dagger worthy of hanging at the king's belt, sire."

Arthur tested the feel of several daggers with elaborate decorative etchings but chose an unadorned weapon that was more balanced.

"You must get close enough to your opponent so thee doth smell his foul breath," Lancelot instructed. Like he'd witnessed in knife fights when he was homeless, Arthur moved forward, holding his dagger below his waist with the blade pointed forward.

"Thou fight bravely with daggers in your dishonorable time?" Lancelot asked.

"Only when we run out of ammunition," Arthur said with a smile.

"Ammunition?"

"What cowards use to harm one another."

"Then, thou knowest to thrust upward rapidly until thy opponent est felled." Lancelot demonstrated in slow motion. Arthur mimicked the moves, then stepped back and sheathed his dagger. "Come at me, knight."

Lancelot didn't understand the slight grin on Arthur's face. "'Tis fraught with danger to even pretend, sire."

As in most rooms in the mansion, Merlin had replaced lamps with candles. Arthur tossed a candlestick to the knight. "Run me through with that."

The knight tentatively jabbed at Arthur.

"No!" Arthur-the-king ordered. "Make it real."

Lancelot shook his head but obeyed, stepping close and thrusting. Arthur deftly blocked the candlestick with his forearm, then flipped the bigger man to the floor. Lancelot jumped up. "Egads, sire. Thou toss me as easily as a stump ball."

"That's how we protect ourselves with karate, a martial art that's even more ancient than your Camelot," Arthur said.

Lancelot had never been so easily controlled by any man. "This hour thou art my tutor."

Lancelot recognized in Arthur an innate instinct for all kinds of fighting. But, more importantly, the teen had a characteristic that Lancelot thought was lacking in modern times: the indomitable heart of a warrior. That elevated him far above ordinary soldiers. Turning the dishwasher into a knight would mostly be a matter of teaching him combat skills and the Code of Chivalry. The wizard's task would be to tutor the young man on how to think and act like a king.

*Arthur stood next to Merlin* in the dining hall, which seemed as vast as a school gymnasium. Modern furniture had been removed and replaced with a rough wooden table at the head of which were two empty thrones. The wizard waved his arm, and a 3D image appeared of lords and ladies in colorful medieval clothes and knights in chain-mail armor gathered in small groups. Life-sized, the people's movements and expressions were realistic, although partially transparent. "The details are authentic," Merlin said. "I attended this very feast."

"Who are these people?" Arthur asked.

"The richest and most powerful nobles in all of England. They are guests of King Uther and Queen Igraine gathered to celebrate the king's Saint's Day at Castle Camelot."

"Is the king in the room?"

"He will enter at his chosen time."

"He sure has lots of friends."

"They cannot be considered 'friends' like you understand friendship, Arthur. They might smile and nod at the king, but they also envy his vast power and wealth. While most do not wish him ill, many are certain they are smarter, bolder, or more judicious, and should rule in his place. They are also his subjects and thus must bow to his will. Your father is a fair and just man who makes decisions that are good for all of England, and he may have angered some of these proud men or made them less wealthy. Today, however, only one actively plots to overthrow the king. Can you spot the traitor?"

By just looking? This was like watching a movie. Maybe if he were actually in the great hall. "Can I enter the vision you've created?"

"Certainly," Merlin said.

"And come back out?"

Merlin nodded. "The ladies may offer a clue. It's not uncommon for wives to have grander ambitions than their husbands and push their men into disloyalty or treason."

Arthur stepped inside the 3D image and realized he was experiencing what it would be like in Camelot 1,200 years ago. The women wore dresses not too dissimilar to modern times, although all had white cloth wrapped around their heads. The men not in armor had on tight leggings with loose thigh-length blouses. Hay was scattered on the floor, but its fragrant scent couldn't disguise the stench of raw sewage. Arthur guessed old-time castles had plumbing issues. On top of that, many of the knights reeked of stale sweat and horse stable stink.

Arthur turned his attention to the ladies. Some had mischief in their smiles. Others posed with heads held high like they owned the joint. A few had watchful, cunning eyes. He then examined the sturdy men with ruddy outdoor complexions. Daggers hung from their belts; some were elaborately carved and decorated with jewels. The nobles' aggressive stances warned of challenging their honor or insulting their horses or women.

The tallest male noble with the most ostentatious dagger was staring at the king's empty throne, arousing Arthur's suspicions. Stepping closer to the man, Arthur smelled a strong odor, like the noble was actively sweating. Did the finely dressed woman he was talking with make him nervous? Or was it his desire to sit on that empty throne?

Suddenly, two massive wood doors banged open, and the king and queen marched in and sat on the thrones. They were followed by armed guards and a pretty young nanny, who had a gap in her front teeth when she smiled lovingly at the baby she carried.

"That infant is *you*, Arthur," Merlin said, pausing the vision.

*Really?* Was he actually there back then? So many things had happened to him lately that his old ways of looking and thinking didn't explain.

Idle chitchat quieted as King Uther and Queen Igraine stared at the assembled guests. Many times Arthur had imagined what his birth parents looked like. But he had never dreamed his father would be so ruggedly good-looking and his mother would glow like a movie star. The longer the silence lasted, the tenser the nobles became. Then, the guards surrounded the tall, fancy-daggered aristocrat and dragged him out. The nobles and ladies avoided looking at the king. Were they next? King Uther beckoned for the nanny to bring him his son. He whispered to the baby. "'Tis often impossible to seeth what darkness lurks in human hearts. Some of my nobles hath genuine affection for the king, and others hath envy and treason behind their smiles. When thou be king, thou mayeth desire to be both loved and feared by your subjects. But, if you cannot have both, 'tis better to be feared."

As suddenly as the 3D scene appeared, it vanished. Arthur's face was scrunched in confusion. *Do I really have to make them fear me?*

After dinner, Arthur flopped onto his bed, his muscles aching and stiff from the sword-fighting practice. He was sure sleep would be instantaneous, but the phrase "loved or feared" kept drowsiness at a distance.

He'd never been in a position where people around him looked to him for direction or judgment. He'd found Ulysses Grant's autobiography in the mansion library and kept it on his bedside table. Arthur lit a candle and reread the passage on how the man led with integrity and modesty. Grant was not vengeful with a defeated enemy and shared the laurels of victory with aides and subordinate commanders. Wasn't this a better way to rule than instilling fear? He fell asleep with the opened book on his lap.

*In his effort to replicate* medieval living conditions, Merlin removed all the modern appliances except two large refrigerators. Geoffrey had to bake in a stone oven and now used a long wooden paddle to pull out a finished loaf. He put the bread on a rough wooden table where Arthur and Lancelot were eating breakfast of cold meat and porridge. Arthur was always hungry here, burning a ton of calories sword fighting. Merlin had explained that old-time castle water was often contaminated, so Arthur washed his breakfast down with ale.

Geoffrey turned a chair around and straddled the seat. "After you guys are through bopping each other on the heads, there's a bar on the commercial strip we passed driving to this monastery where we can knock back a few and hook up with some fine young ladies."

Lancelot ignored this. "We art almost finished with this fine repast, Geoffrey. Bridle and saddle the horses."

"I agreed with Merlin to feed you and the horses. I didn't see any clause in the job description that made me a servant."

"I am knighted. A squire doth ready my steed, and I appoint thee my squire!"

"The only knights we got are the Knights of Columbus, who march in a parade on what used to be called Columbus Day. So you might be a big tuna in Camelot-ville, but you're in Jersey now."

"In Camelot I sliceth off your insulant tongue," Lancelot said.

"That's pretty extreme. I guess they don't have anger management therapy in the seventh century."

# CHAPTER 10

AFTER HER MOTHER DIED, Kate had found at least some comfort strengthening her bond with her grandmother.

Kate visited often, and today when she greeted Agnes, she put on a brave face to disguise her sadness about Art. Then Kate rolled her chairbound grandmother to her favorite sunny spot in the nursing home garden.

Granddaughter and grandmother made every effort not to dwell on Lena's death. Agnes never spoke of enduring a parent's worst nightmare: surviving one of her children. And Kate never talked about the years of financial struggle and emotional distress after her father abandoned the family. Today, Kate told a story about how her mother's boss at the bank's IT department was responsible for Kate getting her own bedroom. Intelligent and hardworking, Lena was promoted over her bullying, lazy, and incompetent superior, and the new position came with a substantial raise. So Kate and her mom had moved from a studio into a two-bedroom apartment. "Thank goodness for incompetence," Kate laughed.

Her lighthearted story didn't fool the ninety-two-year-old, who weighed less than her age and had blue veins showing through her nearly transparent skin. Like her granddaughter, Agnes sensed other people's emotions and thoughts. "Man trouble!" she declared as if that was usually the problem.

Kate told her how Art had left to join what she concluded was a sword-and-sorcery cult.

"At some point, my dear, that kind of man would search for a new shiny idea or woman. I know that doesn't give you comfort today, but it's better that he's gone now than if he'd abandoned you after you were married with a child."

"That would be like repeating what happened to Mom and me."

"Exactly." Agnes touched Kate's arm. "That boy has no sense of purpose in life, my dear. Partners without a crusade diminish you."


*During a pre-breakfast riding lesson* in a newly mown hay field, Lancelot showed Arthur how to loosen the reigns and nudge the horse's side with his heels to lead it from a trot to a faster paced canter. Unlike excellent rider Lancelot, Arthur was awkward but not tense in the saddle for someone who'd never ridden. A cool breeze, not yet scorched by summer heat, invigorated him. Somehow, this rural landscape looked different from the back of a horse. He saw no signs of the modern world: no houses, no electrical power lines, no fences. Only meadows surrounded by woods and stone walls. This could well be what ancient England looked like, and it didn't feel foreign to city-kid Arthur. *Way better than riding the subway.*

They returned to the mansion, slowed to a trot, then dismounted at the stable. "On the morrow, sire, we gallop," Lancelot said.

Like Arthur, the knight usually spoke only when necessary or to offer an insight. So while they didn't engage in small talk or share stories of growing up, Arthur felt a developing bond between him and the knight. He thought that he could trust Lancelot with his doubts.

"Merlin can create images of kings and queens. Do you think they're what really happened back then, or does he create fiction to teach lessons?"

"Even if his stories never happened, they hath truth."

"Merlin told me that after King Uther died, the nobles argued about who should become king. So Merlin created a magnificent sword named Excalibur and buried the blade deep in an iron anvil. Is it true that whoever pulls it free will be the rightful king?"

Lancelot nodded. "Many hath tried and failed to claim the sword and the throne. Only *your* hand as the legitimate king hath the power to possess Excalibur, sire."

Arthur looked at his hands, still red and chapped from scrubbing pots and pans. Could they really have such strength?

After putting the horses in their stalls, he and Lancelot entered the mansion. On the way to the kitchen, Lancelot paused at the small chapel entrance. "Hath thou already recited matins, sire?"

"Matins?"

"Morning prayers."

Arthur shrugged. His foster parents never brought him inside a church or gave him religious instruction. "I don't know about praying."

Lancelot was stunned. A disbeliever? Heretics who doubted religious doctrine were burned alive at the stake in ancient England. "If glorifying God and obeying the Code of Chivalry doth not guide your thoughts and deeds, what doth?"

"Instinct, I guess."

"That is only about thee. Hath thee rules and ideals?"

"Well, a teacher once told me about The Golden Rule. Treat others as you want them to treat you."

The more he learned about life in the present, the more confused

Lancelot became. His religious faith kept him pure. His strict adherence to his code subdued untrustworthy emotions.

He didn't want to challenge his king so kept silent.

Arthur knew that deep inside him, somewhere below his instinct to do good, was his sense that he was destined to fight for something of great importance. Exactly what was still a mystery. But he knew he had to keep moving to find it. Even if it meant his direction would be away from his beloved Kate.


*Sitting on her roof,* Kate promised never to see Art again. But that didn't mean he stopped haunting her. Guys before Art had been gropers, but Art's hands were gentle and knowing. She missed the heat of his body against hers, and how they'd committed to each other so completely that any loneliness evaporated until separate atoms bonded into one.

Rita plunked down next to Kate. "When I didn't find you feeling sorry for yourself in your room, I figured you'd be up here." She offered a slice of pizza. "Want some?"

"I don't have any appetite."

"I wish I didn't."

"I hate myself for missing him."

Rita sensed the unspoken "but" at the end of that sentence. "Hold my ankles, will you? Gotta work off the carbs."

Kate knelt by her friend's feet, pressing down on the ankles. "Remember Barry?" Rita asked as she did sit-ups.

"Yeah. Your ex."

They'd only broken up a few days ago, but Rita didn't have to ask how Kate knew. Her friend sensed things without being told.

"You were in love."

"Yeah, well, Barry-the-bum had a flaw." She exhaled. "I knew he fooled around, but I figured I could persuade him to stop if we got serious. He was faithful for a while, but then it started again. And again. So I fooled around to get back at him. You heard it from me, girl, revenge sex isn't as satisfactory as advertised. This story's moral is that changing guys isn't our job. Even if Art hadn't gone to Neverland with those dudes, it's not part of the deal that you have to make him realize that he's nuts." Rita continued doing sit-ups and grunted, "Love ain't a rehab program."

*Moonlight streaming through his window* transported Arthur to another moonlit night. Kate was snuggled beside me on the lawn at the top of the Great Hill in north Central Park. A full moon cast a haunting blue light, overpowering the harsh glow of the ani-crime sodium-vapor streetlights. *"That's our moon," she said, her husky voice now echoing in my head.*

*"It's ours forever and nobody else's," I replied, and she kissed me.*

Arthur sits up in bed, like he did that night when he and Kate were illuminated by a harsh spotlight attached to a police car stopped on the nearby sidewalk. The late-night quiet was shattered with an amplified voice on the car's loud-hailer, "Okay love-birds, park closes at sunset. Outta here!"

Arthur goes to his bedroom window at the horse farm. The moon sunk below the horizon, and the sky turned into a black hole with no promise of dawn. Arthur stared out at nothingness for what seemed like hours. He woke up his phone to see the screensaver of Kate standing on a rocky hiking trail smiling directly at the camera. He tapped her number and then canceled immediately. *It'll just make me sadder to talk to her.*

His phone rang a few seconds later, and he didn't have to check the incoming number. Kate was the only person in the universe who ever called him.

"You getting up this early or can't sleep?" she asked.

"Can't."

"Me either."

He hadn't planned what he was going to say. "I miss you."

"Don't start, okay?"

She was silent for so long he thought she might have hung up. "You still there?"

"Where did those guys take you?"

"It's pretty fantastic. A horse farm with a mansion."

"In this century?"

That made him smile. "Forsooth, New Jersey. I think it's pretty close to a little town called Lamington. They're teaching …" If he told her they were teaching him to fight with a sword and rule with fear, it would sound crazy. "Freshman orientation start?" he deflected.

"Not yet." She took a long, deep breath. "Look, Art, Arthur. Please don't call me again. I have to go. I've got more crying to do." Then she was gone. He stared at her picture and felt hollowed out inside. *What am I doing here?*

Lancelot *knocked Arthur's sword* out of his hands. "React! You now hath excellent skills. Reason not."

Arthur picked up his sword and rushed forward, yelling loudly to regain his fighting spirit. Lancelot's counterattack made Arthur backpedal to a row of evergreens that formed a windbreak between the mansion and the surrounding pastures. The scent of pine aroused Kate in his brain. *She steps out of the shower, her glowing skin smelling fresh of her favorite evergreen soap.* Lancelot effortlessly knocked Arthur to the ground. "Mort! Mort! Mort!" the knight hollered in French. "What devil hast thy brain?"

Arthur exhaled. "My girlfriend. My ex-girlfriend."

"Adore a maiden. Cherish a maiden. But a warrior cannot allow thoughts of a lady weaken his sword."

"She conquers my thoughts."

"A king doesn't remain king if he be weak."

"Well, maybe I'm not your king. Maybe you got the wrong Arthur."

*Kate couldn't sleep after she and Art … Arthur talked.* How had those two guys brainwashed such a practical, no-nonsense guy who never dreamed of unrealistic futures? Maybe they had him on some powerful mind-altering drug or, worse, were holding him prisoner. In any case, he needed to be rescued.

She climbed out her window to the fire escape and descended to the floor below. It was a steamy morning that promised more breathless heat. Rita rested on top of her bedcovers with only her underwear on. Even so, she was sweating.

Kate stuck her head through the open window. "Hey, girl."

"Hey yourself."

"You got a shift on the bus today?" It made Kate smile that buses are what the EMTs called their ambulances.

"Yeah. Four to midnight."

"So do you mind if I borrow your car?"

"No way. I'm good for five days before moving it for the street sweepers. You're not a true New Yorker if you don't understand a good parking spot's much more important than friendship." She sat up and drank from a glass of water, then her eyes narrowed suspiciously. "Where would you be going in my car?"

"To New Jersey." Kate shrugged. "Just want to look around."

Rita sat on the windowsill next to her friend, unconcerned that prying eyes might ogle a full-figured teenage girl in electric pink underwear. "One of your only failings, Kate, is that you're a terrible liar. Art's out there, isn't he?"

Kate nodded. "Yeah. On a horse farm not too far from the city."

"You know that even the brawniest lifeguard can get sucked under trying to rescue a drowning man who doesn't want to be saved."

"Please don't think I'm weak, okay?"

"I'll never think you're weak." Rita reached inside for the car key on her dresser and hesitated before handing it over. "There are lot of fish in the sea, girl. What about that nice rich kid from your riding camp who has a crush on you? He texts you all the time? You showed me his picture. Cute."

Kate smiled. "Cute's not enough." And she extended her hand for the key.


*Arthur got into the* SUV parked inside the garage. Geoffrey had agreed to drive him back to the city, but nothing happened when he turned the ignition key. "Dang. You know anything about car engines?"

"Not a thing," Arthur said.

Geoffrey tilted his seat back. "You know, all this stuff about being a king and time travel is hard to get your head around. But bro, maybe that's what's real. What if being a fugitive, murdering dishwasher is the unreal part? In the real place, you'll be top dog with people bowing and servants scurrying around to satisfy your most outrageous whims. Back in Camelot-ville, we'll be living large."

"We?"

"What do I have in Present-ville? Every producer on Broadway has rejected the musical I wrote. I'm twenty-six with no apartment or bank account. No woman who loves me and begs me to stay. Where the wizard takes me has to be overflowing with wenches who won't be able to resist my twenty-first-century wit and sophistication."

"Well, I'm not going," Arthur declared and got out of the SUV.

"How're you gonna get to the city? Walk there?"

"Looks like I have to."

Every muscle in his body, every cell in his brain, propelled him toward Kate. Even as king, he felt he would be living half a life without her. She wasn't a sorceress, but he was definitely under her spell, so

Arthur headed out into the drenching rain to beg his soulmate to take him back.

*Kate drove Rita's ten-year-old car* away from a white-columned mansion with a barn big enough for a herd of horses. She stopped where the driveway met the road, pondering which way to go. Heavy rain pelted the metal roof.

High above, thoroughly soaked, angry Crow kept its sharp bird-eyes on the car.

Kate told her phone to call Rita, who answered on the second ring. "Yo, I hope you haven't found him."

"It's a millionaire's horse farm ghetto out here. I've been kicked off of seven estates so far, and still no Art."

"The local cops are going to bust you for DWP."

"What's that?"

"Driving while poor."

"I'll try one more place, and if he's not there, I'll head back."

"How many things have you crashed into?"

"Goodbye, Rita."

Even with her wipers on the highest setting, she could barely see the country road though the rain pelting her windshield. A truck passed in the opposite direction and splashed more water on the windshield, blocking her vision for a second, and she veered to the right. When the water cleared, Kate realized she was about to hit a man walking on the side of the road. He dove out of the way just before the car hit him. Jamming on the brakes, she stopped and ran back to see if the pedestrian was all right. "You okay, mister?"

The man was face down in a muddy puddle, and he slowly got to his knees, his face completely covered with mud. He nodded and used the puddle water to wash off the dirt until his face was recognizable.

"Art!" she yelled.

"Kate!"

"Oh my god, I almost killed you."

She jumped into the puddle and threw her arms around him. "I found you!" she whispered, planting kisses all over his face. "I found my love and I'm never going to let you go."

"I was coming to you."

"Oh, Art," she said, resting her head on his shoulder.

"Enough with this king shit. I was feeling dead inside without you."

"Let's go home."

They got into the car, dripping water all over. Kate put her head on Art's shoulder for a long moment. He reached up and caressed her cheek. "It's you," she whispered.

She started the engine and accelerated, but suddenly, the wheel turned by itself, spinning the vehicle in the opposite direction. "What the hell's happening?" Kate screamed.

She stomped on the brake pedal, but the car didn't slow. She tried to thrust the gearshift into neutral, but it wouldn't budge out of drive.

"I think Merlin's taken control of the car," Arthur said.

"What!? How do we stop him?"

"I don't think we can."

The car turned into the driveway leading to the mansion. "Is this where they've been keeping you prisoner?" she asked.

"The only school I haven't been expelled from," Arthur said. "Knight school. With a K."

Merlin was standing by the front entrance with Lancelot holding a colorful umbrella over his head. The wizard raised his arm and gently moved it to steer the car up the driveway. The rain stopped abruptly, and shafts of sunlight broke through the heavy clouds. For a moment, Arthur wondered if Merlin could control the weather. And had the wizard also arranged this "chance meeting" with Kate? The car stopped in front of the wizard and Lancelot.

Crow spun around and headed back to the city to inform Morgan her victim had traded up from youth shelters and prison to a luxurious mansion in horse country.

Arthur and Kate got out. "Are you some super spy with a device that can take control of a car?" Kate asked Merlin.

Lancelot said, "He est a wizard." *These modern-day people can't be very smart.*

Kate looked at the tall man whose shoulder-length blond hair glistened in the sun. He was so handsome, she caught her breath, and she was a little surprised at herself for that reaction when she was standing next to the person with whom she was desperately in love. Then she focused her thoughts. "There's no Santa Claus, no Easter Bunny, and no wizards."

Lancelot had paid little heed to women in the present time, but there was something wholesome about this one. He bowed extravagantly. "Maybe not in thy world, my lady."

"So are we your prisoners?" Arthur asked angrily.

"If you're a prisoner of anything, Arthur, it's of your blood," Merlin said. "In America today, you have choices. Probably too many. You can attempt a profession you have neither the temperament nor aptitude for. You might fail, but that's not the point. You have the option. But you, Arthur Pendragon, are heir to the throne of Camelot. Being king is your privilege and your destiny."

Kate snorted. "Am I a prisoner too?"

"Now that you're here, you can help Arthur prepare for his responsibility."

"So whatever you madmen are planning to do to Art, you're bringing me along as an ornament and relief for his needs?"

"I promise you'll find important missions in our ancient time, Kate Cambridge," Merlin said calmly.

"Like setting up insane asylums so I can lock you two in a padded cell and throw away the key," she spat out.

# CHAPTER 11

Morgan Le Fay admired herself in the squee-gee-clean glass exterior of the Freedom Tower in lower Manhattan. Modern-day stylish with a new haircut, the sorceress had snipped, accessorized, and sleeveless-sundressed away any evidence she came from a rural country 1,200 years before the invention of spandex.

Crow swooped down to her shoulder, and she brushed the bird to the sidewalk. "Nice do," Crow cawed. "You go to that salon on Madison that only people with $500 for a haircut know exists?"

"Those insolent barbers should have their hands chopped off for treating every woman like royalty."

"Equality, Your Chic-ness. The downside of democracy."

Morgan indicated the tower. "Is this the best mansion?"

"It's certainly the tallest."

"I'll build a new tower at my castle that is this tall. For the queen, size matters."

"Of course. And your most deceitful servant has good news. That adorable young man you want to murder is at a horse farm in New Jersey."

"We'll go there now."

Crow shook its head. "What? No 'well done?' No, 'you deserve a nice dead pigeon'?"

Morgan ignored Crow's questions and shape-changed into a brilliant red cardinal.

"Does red make me look fat?" she asked.

"The color flatters, Your Royal Svelteness, and in New York, you can never be too rich or too thin."

*"Prisoner of your blood? Bullshit!"* Kate growled, her hands balled into fists as she faced Arthur in his bedroom. "You're giving up. You've resigned to the bullshit fate they're feeding you." She swept her arms around the room, indicating the four-poster bed with embroidered canopy and candle instead of an electric lamp on the bedside table. "Look at this ridiculous old-fashioned furniture. It looks like a stage set for a Shakespearean play!"

"Kate ... out here, the reins are loosened and I'm powerful. In the city, I was a mule with a bit in its mouth. Everything and everybody held me back. I couldn't use all my strength and courage there." It was more a declaration than an explanation.

"So what were you doing walking to me in the rain?" she asked. "Were you going to kidnap me?"

"I didn't have a plan."

He reached out, hoping to calm her with a gentle caress, but she swept his hand away, anger blazing from her eyes. "You're not brave enough to face a few years in prison?"

They rarely disagreed and never argued, so they hadn't found ways to modulate or control their heated emotions. Kate immediately regretted her demeaning challenge.

The muscles in Arthur's forearms twitched, and he shifted his weight to the balls of his feet. His fighting stance. "You know what job a convicted murderer gets if they can even find work after prison? Not even a dishwasher!" he shouted. Then, in a soft yet threatening voice, he said, "Don't wish a life without hope on me."

Kate had witnessed Arthur's rage when he encountered bullying or injustice on the city streets, but it had never been directed at her. *He's drowning, and I can't save him without being pulled under myself.*

She was about to apologize, but the damage had been done. Arthur knew it too. "I'll order Merlin not to stop you when you leave." His voice was charged with anger, and he stormed out of the room.

*The king commands. A dagger to the heart. A flashing exit sign.*

*Kate went down the grand,* curved staircase that led to a high-ceilinged dining hall decorated with colorful flags and pennants. Searching for the front door, she entered a long corridor with tapestries depicting ancient kings and queens and armored knights jousting on horseback. *Knights and fair maidens?* Could it be that simple? Half-mature, half-grown men playing knights and kings like nine-year-old boys except with steel swords, not plastic. Sick or harmless, either way, she didn't want any part of it.

She heard the clanking of metal on metal behind a closed door. *Arthur must be lifting weights with angry energy.*

Rita's car was still parked in the driveway, and before Kate could get in, a white snowy owl startled her when it landed on the hood. "Don't be alarmed, Kate. It's me, Merlin." She was even more startled that the bird could talk. "You're not dreaming or hallucinating." The bird shape-changed into Merlin. "It's just an old man with a beard."

Kate looked around, and neither saw nor sensed evidence of staged trickery like a hologram projector. But, of course, a professional conjurer wouldn't be so obvious.

"You know, Kate. You are a chemist and I'm a wizard. We use our skills to combine different elements to make something new, and hopefully, something better. Those mixtures are what you call a covalence bond. It's what you and Arthur have. You are separately strong-willed, courageous, and intelligent individuals, and when you bond together, you amplify each other's strengths to become giants."

"Don't talk to me. You're the one who screwed up Art's mind and split us apart."

"Have you ever considered that I actually *unscrewed* Arthur's mind?"

"You can't be serious." She got partway into the car.

"You wish you had told Arthur that you will always love him," Merlin said.

Kate stopped abruptly and turned back. "You're reading my mind?"

"Yes. Just like you can do."

"You're wrong. I never had that power."

"You deny your power because your science can't explain how you sense people's thoughts."

She could detect Merlin was thinking something, but it was in a foreign language she didn't understand, or maybe in symbols, not words. The next instant, he must have translated his ideas into English because she knew what he was thinking. "*Freak. Isn't that what some people call you due to your powers?*"

*It was true she'd been taunted with that insult and worse.* "Okay, but it's not ESP. It's mostly just guessing by judging body language."

"*You realize this conversation is taking place without either of us speaking? We're transmitting our thoughts to one another.*"

Kate grasped that they were like mimes, with facial expressions amplifying their silent thoughts and emotions. "*Okay. I can read minds. But I hate it.*"

"*Do you wonder if your single-minded devotion to scientific thought is an attempt to deny your extrasensory perception?*"

*"That's absurd."* But could this weird old man be right?

"In your world, modern people do not dare to understand what you are," Merlin said aloud. "Come with us, and you'll be respected for your brilliance in science and ability to read thoughts. We've many who have your talent, and you'll not be a freak."

*"That sounds like one of those dreadful senior-living villages in Florida that my aunt wants to move to."*

Merlin laughed. Somehow, he knew that after her mother's death, Kate had felt like a solitary asteroid so far in deep space that no solar system or planet's gravity pulled her close. Alone. Arthur had changed all that, but his gravity's comforting tug was eliminated when he became part of this cult.

Kate got into the car and was suddenly seized by an overwhelmed dread. It wasn't her life being threatened. It was Arthur's.

She sprinted into the mansion, then flung open the door to the room where Arthur was lifting weights. She was horrified to see him lying on his back on a lifting bench with a heavy barbell pressed against his chest with so much force he couldn't breathe.Veins in his neck bulged, and his arms quivered as he attempted to lift the weights off. A bright red cardinal and a crow were perched on either end of the weights. How could their tiny bird-bodies be applying so much downward pressure?

"Oh my god! Scram!" she yelled, and when the birds didn't move, she tried to swat the crow away, but the cardinal pointed a wing at her, and she froze in place, unable to move.

Merlin entered the room and uttered a terrifying high-pitched scream that drove the birds out an open window. He pointed a finger to unfreeze Kate, then effortlessly raised the barbell and placed it in the metal holding rack above Arthur's head.

"You okay?" she asked Arthur in a weak voice.

He took several deep breaths and nodded as the color gradually returned to his face.

"This is effing wack! A bird tried to kill a human and then somehow paralyzed me, and then you undid it! What the hell is going on?"

"The sorceress Morgan Le Fay shape-changed herself from a human into the red bird and used her powers to increase the weight of the barbell." Merlin explained the unexplainable.

"Sorceress?" Kate asked.

"King Arthur's half-sister. She has time-traveled to kill her rival to rule Camelot."

Things were becoming progressively stranger and weirder. As a scientist, she was surprised that she was curious about what existed at the bottom of a time-travel abyss. But first, she had to revive the teenager with whom she just had a relationship-ending fight.

She pulled Arthur to a sitting position. He stood, a little shaky at first, but his strength quickly rebounded.

"You're not safe from Morgan's attacks," Merlin said. "Until I can put an impenetrable spell on this building, I'll hide you where she can't find you."

"Where's that?" Arthur asked.

"The future. And Kate, you were leaving us, and I won't stop you. But what if Morgan captures you, and you become bait to lure Arthur into a mortal trap?" He paused. "Will you go with him?"

*Surrender to this magic or return to a miserable life without Arthur?* Time-travel to the unknown could be dangerous, even fatal. What if the wizard's powers failed, and she and Arthur became trapped in some dystopian otherworld? The sorceress could time-travel too, so wouldn't she come hunting for them? But the trip into the future promised an adventure on which she could experience new and empowering challenges like her heroine Amelia Earhart. Arthur made her decision easier when he held Kate's hand and whispered, "I love you."

In a clear, firm voice, Kate said, "Yes."

Merlin pointed a finger to shape-change Arthur and Kate into peregrine falcons.

*Whoa! What happened!?* When she raised what were her arms, they were now feathered wings. And while she had the body of a bird, she marveled that she still had her human brain functions and speaking ability.

In a long-ago science class, Kate had learned that some animals, like the golden tortoise beetle and the puffer fish, can shape-change when threatened by a predator. People can alter body shape by dieting or weight lifting but always remain human. She could not think of any scientific explanation for how the wizard had turned her into a bird. *He has to have magic powers.*

"Aren't peregrines the fastest flying birds?" peregrine Arthur asked.

"Faster than time," Merlin said, pointing out the window. "Fly wherever your whims lead into the future. At dawn, turn around and return. That will give me time to create defenses Morgan cannot penetrate."

Arthur flew out the open window and rapidly gained altitude. Kate followed, testing her wings tentatively, then boldly exerting more power to accelerate with jet-plane-takeoff speed. An unseen updraft lifted them effortlessly higher. Soaring high above the earth, she felt an exhilarating freedom! AMAZING!

Arthur flew next to her. "Sorry for getting angry."

"Back at ya."

"Oh, and thanks for saving my life."

"I was saving my life too, because I won't live without you."

"Come on!" Arthur headed straight down to test his speed. Kate pulled her wings close to her body and dove. She remembered reading that peregrines could fly over 200 miles per hour, and this plummeting dive was so thrilling fast, she must be going close to that speed.

They avoided crashing into the ground by turning upward so close to the earth that Kate's wings brushed tree leaves. Arthur streaked in a tight circle around Kate, who immediately gave chase. In a bloodless joyful dogfight, they spun and tumbled through the air, exuberant warplanes with feathers.

Kate had fantasized about flying solo, but that was at the controls of an airplane. She never imagined becoming a bird seemingly free from gravity's insistence. But here she was, soaring with no fears, no doubts. She wanted more if this was how magical experiences made her feel.

She flew close to Arthur, touching his wing with hers. "This isn't as good as making love with you," she said over the whisper of rushing wind, "but it's real close."

"Shall we do a comparison test later?"

"Absolutely!"

Their telescoping peregrine eyes could see tree leaves far below turning brilliant reds and oranges as they flew from summer into fall. Then they entered nighttime. The stars seemed close and friendly, elevating Arthur's mood further until he spotted a group of buildings with barred windows.

"Is that a prison?" Kate asked.

"Yeah. Look at all that razor wire. This is where murdering teenagers get locked up," Arthur said.

In an outdoor area lit by harsh orange light, they could see a young guy fighting three others simultaneously. "The solo guy looks like you," she said. "How long can he keep those other boys away?"

"This has to be a warning from Merlin. He is hiding us in the future but isn't going to miss the chance to remind me what'll happen if I stay in the present."

"Can we help him? Can we help you?" Kate asked, indicating the solo fighter.

"No, we can't interfere."

They flew on, heading for a glow that illuminated the night horizon. "Maybe my future's there in that city," Kate said.

Soon, they flew into New York, zipping between and around tall skyscrapers at full speed like they were inside a video game. Then, Kate slowed and hovered over the street where her aunt's apartment was. A van with "Sunshine State Movers" written on the side was pulling away from the curb. She soared past the apartment's unlit windows and landed on the sidewalk next to a pile of clothes. Arthur alighted next to her and recognized Kate's scarf.

"Pretty bleak," Kate said. "What do you think? We've traveled about a year into the future?"

"Could be. This is your stuff?"

"Yeah. Angry Ant must be moving to her retirement hell and tossed my clothes here."

"So you won't have a place to live in New York. This must be Merlin's version of your future here."

Kate retrieved her mother's silk scarf with her beak, and Arthur used his beak to wrap the scarf around her bird neck. "I've seen enough of this future shit," Kate said.


*The eastern sky was blushing red* as dawn approached. They flew back in time toward the horse farm. Now the forest leaves turned from brilliant fall colors to deep summer green. The peregrines landed by the mansion pool, where Merlin looked up from his cell phone to shape-change them into humans.

"That was amazing!" Arthur was glowing.

Kate unknotted her handkerchief and tugged it with both hands to ensure it was real. Physical proof she had time-traveled.

"I've conjured an invisible protective shield around the house that Morgan Le Fay cannot penetrate," Merlin told them, "but when you are outside, you must be armed and alert."

Kate and Arthur went into the weapons room. "No pink daggers for the ladies?" Kate kidded.

"I think only knights carried weapons back then," Arthur said.

"What? Am I supposed to defend myself by scratching this Morgan character with my fingernails?" Kate chose a dagger with ornate etching and strapped it to her waist. "Medieval women's lib."

They went back outside onto a large stone patio. It was a brilliant, cloudless morning. Hot, but not humid. Arthur warily looked for any sign of the sorceress, and Kate didn't sense danger. She did spot a pedestal and, pointing to twelve roman numerals around its circular edge, said, "A sundial. Sort of a clock."

"I can't think that would be very accurate."

"Not by modern standards." She ran her finger over the vertical metal triangle in the middle of the numbers. "But I know how and why it works. The sun's rays are made of tiny packets of energy called photons. This triangle interrupts the photons to create a shadow that indicates the approximate time. This happens today and always because of nature's irrefutable and eternal laws. So being transformed into a falcon and flying into the future is like discovering Santa Claus is real." She paused. "A brilliant guy in my internship lab is a fundamentalist Christian. If he can reconcile his belief that God created the world in seven days with his science, I guess I can believe in science and magic at the same time."

She turned to face Arthur and took both his hands in hers. "I'd thought I'd lost the love of my life forever and now we're together. That's another kind of magic."

# CHAPTER 12

KATE HEFTED A BARBELL above her head in the horse farm exercise gym, where Arthur taught Lancelot karate.

"You go, girl," Arthur encouraged.

"Kate hath the strength of a man," Lancelot said.

He and Arthur were protected by foam-covered helmets and boots. "Keep your weight centered, then spin and kick at the same time," Arthur said. "I'll do it in slow motion."

Bouncing on the balls of his feet, Arthur spun counterclockwise and jumped, kicking toward Lancelot's head but deliberately not landing the blow. Arthur motioned for the knight to try, and he athletically mimicked his teacher's moves.

"Nice," said Arthur. "Tell me, is there single combat in Camelot?" Arthur asked.

"Most certainly. Jousting. Though more sport than battle. But such exhilaration!"

They exchanged several mock blows as Arthur demonstrated different attack and defense techniques. "Long ago, more ancient than your time, Lancelot," Arthur said, "the Greeks were battling Trojans, and neither side was winning. So, a mighty Trojan warrior challenged the Greeks to send out their best fighter for single combat. The victor would determine which side won the war. Very cool."

"Eleven!" Kate bellowed as she completed one more lift. Dropping the heavy barbell onto the floormat, she flashed an I-did-it smile.

"Which knight triumphed?" Lancelot asked.

"Neither. They fought for many days, but neither could defeat the other. The warriors were so impressed with the other's skill that they exchanged gifts."

Kate bounced over to the guys. "Ready?"

"For what?" they asked.

"To get your butts kicked." She spun and kicked as they did. Only Arthur's lightning reflexes enabled him to block her foot from hitting his temple. "You've been practicing."

Kate grinned. "I wish I'd known how to do this when I went on a date with that creep Howard what's-his-name."

Merlin came in with his cell phone light on. "Does anyone know why my lab's lamps have gone black?"

"Maybe a circuit breaker tripped," Kate said. "Let's see if we can find the panel box."

Merlin tilted his head sideways. "Circuit breaker? Panel box?"

"Let's take a look," Kate said. She located the electrical panel in the hallway near Merlin's workspace and ran her index finger along the circuit breakers until she found the one that had popped open. "Here's the culprit." She pushed it to close the circuit.

Merlin saw light now radiating out of his workspace. "You know about this electricity magic, Kate?"

"The wiring in our old apartment was so bad, the breakers were always flipping. I learned from watching Mom."

"Will you advise me about this magic?"

"You're the wizard."

"About turning people into toads. Not electricity."

He led her into his lab, crammed with a portable X-ray machine, a radio-controlled race car, and other gadgets. He showed her a circle of devices surrounding the blue sapphire he wore around his neck.

"These boxy things are electrical magnets," he said, turning one on. Loose pens, paper clips, and other metal flew through the air and clunked against the metal face. "I'm experimenting with magnetism. It's a kind of magic I don't understand."

"Wait. You turned the electrical magnets on all at once?"

"Yes."

"That explains it. Everything all on at once overloaded the circuit, and the breaker popped to prevent the wires from overheating."

"So if I wanted to experiment with more powerful magnets, would that be possible?"

"Probably not here. I don't think there's enough electricity from power lines on the street. But at school where I have a chemistry internship, there's a lab where they're working on nuclear fusion. The magnetic field is how they contain the fuel, I think. Anyway, it's one of the strongest magnets in America, but access is super restricted."

*Modern times have produced many miracles, and one of them is that bright young women don't have to fake fainting spells or do needlepoint as they do in Camelot. They can be curious and competent like Kate Cambridge.* "Have you ever been to England?"

"No. Why?"

"I'm going to show you something."

Merlin waved his arm to create an image of a small city seen from above. Kate and Merlin had a bird's-eye view of the churches and stone buildings around grassy courtyards.

"Do you know where we are?" he asked

"I'd guess we're over a college town."

"This is modern-day University of Cambridge in England."

She smiled. "Like my name."

"What if a brilliant, strong-willed woman didn't go to Camelot? What if someone named Kate Cambridge established a university twelve hundred years ago and then, later, her descendants moved that institution to the village of Cambridge where great poets, scientists and scholars now thrive? Wouldn't it be more fulfilling to create one of the world's greatest learning centers than sitting in a chemistry lab all day to inch modern-day science forward?"

Somehow, he knew she wondered if her life would be diminished in Camelot. Kate understood Merlin was a good magician and now, a good salesman—alerting her to the progressive things she could achieve in ancient England. Merlin had found the spot in her inner being that wanted to create something important and meaningful.

# CHAPTER 13



THE WIZARD WAS BENT OVER A TABLE when Arthur entered the lab.

"Have you looked in the mirror lately?" Arthur asked. "Your hair and beard are turning brown."

"Ah, yes. I had anticipated I might experience reverse aging since it happened when I time-traveled here with you seventeen years ago." He grinned, and his teeth were no longer rotting yellow. "The sap's rising again."

What Merlin didn't tell Arthur was that as he was getting younger, his powers were diminishing. The blue sapphire's inner radiance hanging around his neck had faded, and its ability to augment the wizard's magic had started to dwindle.

Arthur indicated a machine. "Is this the thing you told me can make jewelry out of nothing?"

"Yes, that's a 3D printer. A modern-day alchemist. It can't change lead into gold but can make beautiful objects from Resin Number 40."

"Beautiful is good."

At *Arthur's request*, Geoffrey prepared Kate's favorite meal, rainbow trout roasted with fresh herbs. After dinner, Arthur and Kate walked hand in hand around the picturesque property. It was a cool night with no moonlight so the stars were a brilliant carpet above them. Kate traced the Big Dipper constellation with her finger and ended at the brightest star at the end of the handle. "Enslaved people in the South before the Civil War called the Big Dipper the drinking gourd, and the two stars on the Dipper's cup led to Polaris, the North Star. When they escaped from the plantations, the slaves used that star to guide them north to freedom," Kate said. *Where will that star lead me?*

"How do you like it here at the farm?" he asked.

"Using candles instead of electric lights is sort of romantic, but there's no romance in

the bathroom. A wooden commode with a hole in the seat and a bucket underneath. No flush toilet. No toilet paper. Just cloth strips for cleaning up. Yuk. And the bag with rose petals hanging nearby didn't mask the odor."

"Merlin has staged this whole thing so it's like living in a Middle Ages castle."

"It's different, all right. Halfway between sleepaway camp and what I imagine a prison work farm is like."

"You don't like it then?"

"Where we are isn't important."

"What is?"

"Being with you."

At the horse farm without Kate, he was gaining physical strength and prowess with weapons and riding, but his preoccupation with his lost love made him potentially vulnerable as a warrior and less insight-ful as a king. With her beside him, though, his energy was boundless. His mind was more focused that it had ever been.

He'd prepared for this moment by searching the internet in Merlin's lab for the right words and phrases, but he still swallowed hard. Taking a slow breath, he said, "Kate." She turned to him and he knelt. "Kate … will you … will you marry me?"

The suddenness of his proposal surprised Kate. Getting married was something way down the road. Maybe after college, but most likely after she got a PhD. She was only seventeen. What if she fell in love with someone with the same intensity as her emotion for Arthur like Rita had suggested? Like the riding camp boy. Had her attraction to Lancelot allowed that thought to sneak into her head?

Kate wasn't sure how to answer Arthur. Her grandmother sensed things about people. Maybe Agnes's reaction to Arthur would help Kate decide. "Will you meet my grandmother?" she asked.

Her hesitancy became clear. An audition, he realized. *Strong-willed, independent Kate needed affirmation that she was making the right decision.* "Has your grandmom liked your boyfriends before me?"

"You're my first."

"And hopefully your last."

Geoffrey drove everyone into Upper Manhattan where Agnes Cambridge lived in a nursing facility.

He parked out front and Kate and Arthur got out, followed by Lancelot and Merlin who were guarding them.

"Not all grownups like me."

"We'll see, won't we." Kate took Arthur's trembling hand. "Anxious to make a good first impression?" She arched an eyebrow and smiled. "That's cute in a king."

*Arthur and Kate sat across a table* from Agnes Cambridge on the nursing home patio, surrounded by gardens of colorful flowers and a pink-blossomed cherry tree in full bloom. Some elderly residents wore winter coats, though they sat in direct sun. Dressed in contemporary clothes, Merlin and Lancelot stood guard not far away. Arthur detected steel behind Agnes's watery blue eyes. She flashed a smile, partially taming the butterflies fluttering in his stomach.

"May I hold your hand?" she asked him.

"Of course."

She cradled his hand in hers. "So warm. I imagine mine feel like there's not much life in them."

Her skin was cold, but Arthur had not yet sworn the knight's oath to tell the truth, so he smiled reassuringly. "They feel just fine."

"You don't talk idly or nervously. That's an excellent trait. And I sense you're confident and strong enough not to fear being gentle. Besides, you're kinda sexy. It's easy to understand why Kate loves you."

He smiled. "Thank you, Ms. Cambridge."

"Those two men look like they are watching over you. Are you an important person?"

"Not yet."

"I like that answer, Arthur. Will you excuse us for a moment? I have some things to discuss with Kate."

*Did I pass the audition?* "Certainly."

He went inside, followed by his bodyguards.

"He has asked you to marry him," Agnes said.

"Yes."

"But you haven't responded to his proposal."

"I will soon."

"If you weren't so wise, I'd say you're too young to marry. But from this brief meeting, I know Arthur has strengths that you do not, and you have abilities and insights that he has yet to learn. Together, you will be a magnificent union heightening each other's best qualities."

"Thank you, Grandmom. You're the best."

"And he's going to take you to a distant place."

"Yes. So far that I won't be coming back."

Agnes spotted tears in Kate's eyes. "You're an adventuress, so you must go on that voyage. Don't worry about me. I'm not alone. Richard on my floor can still stand up straight and reads me trashy novels. He's a pretty good kisser too. Maybe because he's only eighty-six."

Kate figured her grandmother was making this up so she wouldn't feel bad about leaving. "I'm sure no man can resist you, Grandmom."

Agnes took off a locket hanging around her neck. It had two faces, one smiling and one sad. "This belonged to my mother. She was independent and strong-willed, just like another Katherine I know." She nodded at Kate. "Mother was an actress—in the days when respectable women didn't join theatrical troupes—that traveled around the country performing farces and tragedies. Sometimes the companies went bankrupt in places like Butte, Montana. This was way before credit cards or cell phones to call for help." She pressed the clasp, and inside the small compartment was a blue sapphire. "Katherine carried this locket for such an emergency. She could sell the valuable gem to get money for train fare back to New York City, where she lived. She gave it to me before she died." Kate sensed a wave of sadness crash over her grandmother. "I don't have many regrets, but I'm sad I never got to give this to Lena. The accident took her so suddenly." Agnes handed the locket to her granddaughter. "If you're ever stranded where it seems impossible to find a way home, this gem will get you there."

Kate and her grandmother exchanged hugs and goodbyes with no tears. Then Kate joined Merlin and Lancelot, who were stationed outside the men's bathroom.

"Is Arthur in there?" she asked.

They nodded. Kate barged through the door just as Arthur was washing his hands. "Yes!" She jumped up, wrapping her legs around his waist. "I'll marry you wherever you are! Whenever you are!"

# CHAPTER 14

GEOFFREY DROVE EVERYONE into New York City and then brought them back to the horse farm way after midnight.

It was the first night Kate and Arthur shared a bed, but both of them were so physically and emotionally exhausted, they fell asleep in one another's arms.

Kate stirred awake when sun was just poking over the horizon. Arthur's side of the bed was empty, the sheets not even warm, so he had been up for a while. She dressed, then caught sight of herself in a mirror. Just like her grandmother, she didn't use makeup. Agnes had once told her, "You have enough natural beauty that you don't have to paint over it." Even if she used eyeliner or lipstick, these would likely go on clown-crooked because of the distorted image in the Middle Ages-era mirror that had an uneven surface. She had to chuckle. *Life outside New York City was different!*

The clang of metal on metal interrupted her musing. Out her window, she spotted Arthur and Lancelot sword-fighting on the lawn. Not wanting to miss out on the fun, she ran to the weapons room and grabbed a heavy two-handed broadsword.

*Near the pool, Arthur and Lancelot* were squatting. Both men wore padded protective clothing and had pulled off their helmets, their hair matted with sweat.

Kate charged up brandishing her sword. "The damsel's here to save the knights in distress!"

Arthur laughed as heartily as she had ever heard, but Lancelot cocked his head in confusion. Kate had the confident bearing of the noble class, but a well-bred woman would never wield a broadsword. He was sworn by the Code of Chivalry to protect maidens. Still, even in jest, this lady appeared determined to defend herself. He was pleasantly surprised that this new idea appealed to him. "Wence misfortune doth arise, I shalt call for thy assistance," he said without irony.

"What are you guys up to? Or down too, really?"

"Lancelot has been teaching me how to endure a sword blow. So I'm showing him how I learned to endure pain in karate," Arthur said. "This position is called *kiba dachi*, the horse's stance."

"Much more fun than sunning by the pool," Kate kidded and squatted in between them.

The minutes went by slower and slower as the pain built up in their thigh muscles and lower backs. They all tried to maintain oh-this-ain't-nothin' faces, but the grimaces slowly took over. And the grunts. Everyone's muscles began to twitch, but no one wanted to be the first to give in.

Geoffrey came by carrying dead rabbits and a basket of greens and shook his head. "You having a taking-a-dump contest, or what?"

He held up the rabbits. "Freshly killed bunnies and wild ramps for dinner. And lighten up on that macho shit." When he headed toward the mansion, he deliberately stumbled into Kate, knocking her over into Arthur, who tumbled against Lancelot. They all lay on their backs, shaking off the stiffness in their thighs.

"I went down first, so I guess I lost," Kate laughed.

"That servant is an insolent lout!" Lancelot grumbled. "He deliberately pushed you over."

"I'd had enough fun," Kate said.

They all got up, and Kate high-fived Arthur. "Here's to horse asses."

Lancelot elaborately knelt before her. "The king sayeth you shalt marry, Your Royal Majesty."

"Rise, Sir Knight, and no more Royal Majesty queen stuff. Just plain Kate'll do fine."

"The bards sayeth there est nothing plain about Your Majesty," Lancelot said.

*Is he flirting, or is this more old-time chitchat?*

As they all walked toward the house, Lancelot described life in Camelot, a splendid walled city with a magnificent castle. The knight was not usually so vocal, and Kate was impressed by his solemn eloquence as he praised the comradeship among the devout knights, who prayed daily and celebrated saints' days. He was positively exuberant about the glorious jousting tournaments. It was almost like he was creating a poem about an ideal world where chivalry, courage, honor, loyalty, and faith existed purely and unchallenged.

Kate could see that Arthur was completely entranced, like a kid hearing stories of the magic of Disney World.

Arthur flung his arm around Lancelot's shoulder with easy affection. Kate knew that in the city, in the shelters, Art ... Arthur ... had been a loner who'd stopped trying to make friends because kids came and went so quickly. It pleased Kate that he found someone like Lancelot, a young man of equal strength and shared values, to be his companion.

*An actor in high school musicals,* Geoffrey enthusiastically cast himself in the role of seventh-century chef. His costume, provided by Merlin, was a medieval-era cloth hat decorated with a pheasant's feather and a wide leather belt that barely contained the enormous globe of his belly. And the farmhouse kitchen was his stage. As he slathered butter over rabbits roasting on a spit, he sipped a honey-based alcoholic drink he'd concocted.

Kate and Arthur sometimes joined him for meal preparation. Today, Kate was dicing shallots with a crude kitchen knife, and Arthur was washing a greasy fry pan in a tub of soapy water when Lancelot came in wearing his chain-mail armor. "Sire, a peasant's labor is not for the king!"

"Maybe Arthur'll bring some modern democratic sensibility to governing," Kate said with a smile.

"If this democracy causeth all the godliness in your modern world, I pray it stayeth here."

"Okay, okay," Arthur said, drying his hands and straightening his shoulders. "I shalt claim my throne," he pronounced, and sat on a kitchen stool.

Lancelot curiously inspected Geoffrey's camera that was on the kitchen counter. "Est this a pagan religious relic?"

"It's the instant camera I used to take your picture in my SUV," Geoffrey said. "Look through the glass piece and press the red button on the front to take a picture of anything you want."

The knight pointed the camera at Kate and pressed the button without releasing pressure, and she vamped. As the pictures popped out, Geoffrey picked them up and spread them out on a cutting board. Big-smiling Kate, pouting Kate, jester Kate with the kitchen knife between her arm and chest with only the handle showing, and serious brow-knitted Kate, whose perceptive eyes focused on the photographer.

"The camera loves Kate!" Geoffrey said and claimed the jester for himself. Arthur liked the smiling Kate photo. She chose the pouty one, saying the young lady with the thoughtful stare was "running for class president." Lancelot selected serious Kate because it captured her essence.

*Now that Kate had decided* to be his queen, Arthur could focus more completely on his instruction. Though he wasn't sure how a board game would teach him about ruling a kingdom, he was confident there was wisdom in Merlin's methods. Arthur committed to learning the strategy and tactics of chess, and after dinner, he and Merlin played a game in the library. Kate was watching the game in progress but didn't want to disturb Arthur's concentration, so she joined Lancelot, arranging toy soldiers and knights on horses into opposing armies on a nearby table.

The wizard had counseled Arthur that just as he had to anticipate his opponent's next move, he needed to predict what action or series of steps an opposing army or treacherous noble would most likely take to harm or kill the king.

Merlin put his finger on his chess queen. "I can take your castle in three moves. How can you save it?" Arthur couldn't remember when he'd ever concentrated with such consuming intensity. *I'm bulking up my brain.*

"I don't see how," Arthur said.

"It's late and you're tired. Study the board with rested eyes tomorrow until you figure it out."

This mental exertion exhausted Arthur much more than the marathon sword-fighting sessions. But he would not retreat due to fatigue and continued to contemplate his next moves.

Kate knew he would not stop until he fell asleep with his head on the table or solved the challenge. She turned to Lancelot. "Did you train to become a knight like you and Merlin are training Arthur?"

"Yes, Your M—"

"Kate!"

He could not force himself to say her name. "Royalty shalt be always addressed with proper title and respect."

"How about Queen Kate."

He thought about this for a moment, then nodded.

"Do all young men become knights?" she asked.

"Sons of nobles and titled families hath the opportunity. Not all hath sufficient will or faith."

"Did you have those traits, or did your instructors instill them in you?"

They'd not spoken often, and he'd always been formal and somewhat stiff with Kate, like he was reciting from a handbook on how to talk to a lady. But now, realizing she was genuinely curious, he relaxed and became almost poetic as he described how knights in training started in their young teens as squires or servants to a warrior already knighted by the king. "We doth care for our knight's horses, armor, and weapons, learneth to faithfully honor and obey the Code of Chivalry. 'Tis a blessing that Merlin tutored me in Latin and French."

Initially, Kate had thought Lancelot was a muscle-bound dolt. But the enthusiasm with which he described the idyllic, uncomplicated adventure of becoming a knight warmed her to this stilted young man. And the way he'd recited the lyrics from a medieval song about the wonders of Old England, called "Land of Hope and Glory," entranced her.

"Yes!" they heard Arthur shout, and he walked to where the toy soldiers were laid out. "The only way of winning was to sacrifice my bishop. Then I was able to capture his king," he said with a grin, showing them a chess piece king. Then Arthur used the chess piece to knock over one of Lancelot's toy foot soldiers. "King takes pawn," he joked.

Kate smiled, but Lancelot remained stone-faced. Arthur realized he'd never seen the knight joke or make frivolous or insincere remarks. Maybe for the knight, joking diminished his faith and tainted his sworn oaths.

"You just killed one of your pikemen, sire," the knight said.

Arthur stood the toy soldier upright. "Is this another game like chess?"

"'Tis the formation King Uther used to siege and defeat the rebel Welsh king and his army."

Arthur knew he wasn't returning to Camelot to play-act king. Instead, he had a mission to defeat Morgan Le Fey, a cause much more significant than anything he'd ever dreamed he could accomplish. He put the chess king on the table in front of the rest of the soldiers. "Warrior kings led from the front."

Lancelot nodded in approval.

Kate sensed Arthur's acceptance of his responsibility as king was already amplifying his resolve and expanding the dimension of what he could accomplish. She could see it in the confident way he was standing.

*Lancelot was teaching the rookies* how to joust, explaining that two warriors charged at each other from opposite directions using lances to knock their opponent off his horse. To develop this technique, Arthur and Kate practiced the technique by aiming their long lances at a knight's shield attached to a wooden swivel. Arthur cantered his horse toward the target. On their horses, Lancelot and Kate watched Arthur miss the mark and then angrily return to the starting point.

Kate urged her horse into a full gallop and charged forward. Many summers at horse camp made her an excellent rider. As tall as Arthur and naturally strong, she had no trouble controlling the heavy lance. She hit the shield's center, making it spin around the pole on its swivel, then guided her horse back to Arthur and Lancelot.

"Perfect," Lancelot said. "Again."

Arthur dutifully charged and this time hit the target.

"Now, Queen Kate. Once more."

Kate made a face. "I'm hot and drenched in sweat. Just as you stinky dudes are. Enough!" Spurring her horse's flanks, she sped toward the target. But instead of attacking it, she flung the lance to the ground and galloped away from them, looking back with a mischievous smile. Arthur immediately chased her. Lancelot hesitated, but realizing that students didn't automatically obey their tutors in this strange modern world, he spurred his horse forward.

The low, rolling hills and flat pastures surrounding the horse farm were ideal for galloping. Arthur had become more comfortable in the saddle, and the joy of speed made him forget all the frustration of the lance drill. Kate dropped her reins, leaned back in her saddle, and spread her arms as if attempting to fly. Her horse slowed enough that Arthur caught up to her and whooped with joy. A few moments later, Lancelot galloped up to ride on her other side, and the serious knight wore a smile.

They thundered by Merlin with the black bear he had tamed, and the animal was using its claws to dig for roots Merlin wanted for potions. The wizard looked up and grinned with delight to see such exuberant camaraderie.

Suddenly, a breeze carried the hint of silphium, alerting him that Morgan was near. Merlin hopped on the bear's back to chase the riders.

Kate, Art, and Lancelot passed a wooded area where the trees had thick, leafy branches. The foliage provided cover to hide the black crow but not the iridescent parrot beside it.

Kate sensed the presence of the sorceress. "Morgan's close! We have to get inside the mansion now!" she yelled.

A waist-high stone wall blocked their way, and Kate skillfully guided her horse over it. Not far behind, Lancelot did the same. She looked back, concerned that rookie horseman Arthur might not know how to handle the obstacle.

As Arthur approached the wall, the parrot pointed a bright wing at him. Instead of leaping, his horse planted its forelegs in the soft earth, launching Arthur headfirst toward the stones.

Racing up on the bear, Merlin pointed his arm to levitate Arthur, allowing him to clear the wall and land feet first. But his momentum carried him forward, and he flipped onto his back in tall grass to slow down. Kate and Lancelot jumped off their horses to check on him. "I keep having to ask if you're okay!" she panted.

Arthur grimaced. "Man, I felt like I was elevated over that wall!"

"I saw Merlin use his magic," Kate said.

In the tree, Crow said, "It was an elegant plan, Your Flamboyantness. I don't know how cute boy survived."

"That damn Merlin protected him," the parrot answered in Morgan's voice. "But not for long."

Crow arched a crow eyebrow. *The magician's not doing too badly so far.*

# CHAPTER 15

IN THE HORSE FARM LIBRARY, Merlin magically conjured a 3D moving image of a castle's great hall. A king and a queen presided at the head of a long table around which nobles, knights, a cardinal, and two bishops gathered.

"Welcome to Camelot," Merlin announced.

Arthur was sitting on a sofa and studied every detail. The knight and some nobles wore chain-mail armor and tunics embroidered with emblems or family crests. The priests with gold pointed hats had cloaks decorated with gold threads. Knights in full armor holding lances with colorful banners stood in a circle around the table. The king's clothes were lined with pure white fur, and the queen wore a bright green dress.

Lancelot fidgeted in a reading chair near the sofa, his eyes riveted on Kate. Many beautiful maidens had unashamedly flirted with him at his father's castle, but they didn't listen to him as if they were interested in every word he said the way Kate did. None had ever excited in him a never-before-felt desire as she did. And he wasn't at all certain that was a good thing.

He quickly looked away when she met his gaze and smiled.

Sitting next to her future husband, she had an unexpected thought: *It's not fair that any young man could be so gorgeous.*

Merlin delighted in using a handheld laser pointer to indicate the apparitions' identities. "That's the chamberlain who runs the castle. Next is the Chancellor of the Exchequer, who collects taxes and procures supplies. Then, the Minister of War. On the thrones, King Uther and Queen Igraine."

The king had a high forehead, dark-brown hair, and a prominent chin. His eyes were winter-sky blue, and the queen's were electric green.

"Your mother's beautiful!" Kate said.

Arthur straightened to sit tall like the king who radiated assurance without an arrogant sneer or haughty glare. "Why is the seat next to the king empty?" Arthur asked.

"That is for his most trusted advisor, the Hand of the King. Uther was unsatisfied with his former Hand and dismissed him and today he will appoint a new one. The nobles and priests have conspired to become the replacement and are anxious to hear his choice."

The king unscrolled a document and began to read.

"What does the king proclaim, Arthur?" Merlin asked.

"I don't know. He's reading in a foreign language."

"Official documents in Camelot were written in Latin. You'll have to learn it to ensure the laws you decree are written as you command. Or have someone you trust without reservation to translate for you." Merlin continued, "The king has declared that Igraine is now not only queen, but she'll also be Hand of the King."

Kate was impressed by how Igraine strode purposefully to the minister's empty chair, which she turned upside down on the table.

Then the queen sat on her throne, looking straight into the king's eyes, not as an inferior needing approval, but as an equal.

Understanding the sly wizard's methods, Arthur said, "That's why you brought us to this moment and this decision in ancient Camelot. To witness the king and the queen becoming a team."

"Every moment in life is a learning experience, Your Majesty."

Arthur nodded. "Camelot will need fierce Lancelot to be Minister of War." The knight bowed. "Thou honoreth me, sire." Arthur continued. "And for the Hand of the King ..." He reached out and took Kate's hand.

*Arthur and Kate were still holding hands* as they exited the mansion into a glorious summer night. The cloudless sky was a sparkling dome, and a gentle breeze shooed away the mosquitos. Daggers attached to their belts, they looked around for any signs of Morgan Le Fay. "I don't sense the sorceress," Kate said. "Want to swim?"

Not waiting for his answer, she ran to the pool, stripped to her underwear, and jumped in. Arthur did the same.

A short time later, Lancelot came outside, and when he saw them splashing joyfully, he discreetly hid behind some hedges. He was still near enough to help if they needed his protection.

Arthur and Kate swung each other around and around in the pool's shallow end. Then, they stopped and leaned against the pool's edge to gaze at the stars.

The underwater lamps illuminated their bodies in a shimmering glow. Lancelot had never seen a woman who wasn't fully clothed, nor had he even imagined what any of the young maidens he idolized would look like naked. Could he worship Kate now that she had undressed in front of a man? The courageous knight who had never retreated in battle wanted to flee from temptation and forget everything he had witnessed. But his duty to guard the king was paramount, so he stayed.

"Someone could say I'm a little underqualified for this king thing," Arthur mused.

"You got da blood, homie," Kate said. "Besides, you learned dishwashing on the job. Figuring out how to king people can't be more complicated than that," she kidded.

He laughed, then stopped. "I saw you and Lancelot eyeing each other. Do you think he is handsome?"

"You're the handsome one. He's almost *too* pretty."

Arthur wasn't sure if she was making a compliment or a criticism.

She and Arthur pulled Styrofoam noodles off the pool apron and began to aimlessly float around.

"Does it make you sad that you never knew your parents?" she asked. "Why?"

"Just wondering what you would ask them if you could?"

Arthur didn't answer for a long time. "I'd want to know why my father sent me to a place where I would learn nothing about how to rule or become a great warrior. I'm not happy he cheated on my mother if this Morgan Le Fay is my half-sister. I'd want to know why he fired his Hand of the King. And I'd ask my mother why she agreed to send her son away. Tell me, Kate, why would a mother give up her baby for someone else to raise?"

"That's hard to answer. Maybe if she was certain the baby wouldn't survive in Camelot." She paused. "Didn't your foster parents explain who you were and why you were in the present?"

"Either they didn't know or didn't care to tell me. Nothing I did ever pleased them, so we didn't talk much."

"Sounds like they didn't show much love or support."

He laughed bitterly.

"I guess that makes you a kind of an orphan. Like me. After my mother died, I felt this giant uncertainty because no one thought I was worthy of being loved." She kissed him tenderly. "But you chased that uncertainty out the door, you big hunk."

"I was just a going-nowhere dishwasher until you loved me."

"You were never just a dishwasher." She sweeps her arm around to indicate the horse stables and mansion. "As we have pleasantly discovered."

Again, he was thoughtfully quiet. "What would you want to know from your father if you ever met?"

"He abandoned my mother and me when I was two, and I've got absolutely zero interest in a selfish lowlife who would do that to his family. Anyway, I think he died."

"How about visiting his grave?"

She blew out a breath that sounded like a curse and shook her head. "No."

"I'll visit my parents' graves when we get to England."

"Kings and queens don't get planted in the ground. They'll have a mausoleum or grand tombs. Do you think seeing them might clarify some of your mixed emotions for them?"

He nodded. Then, he slapped the water's surface to make a loud splash. "But why are we talking about resentfulness? We're young and in love, and we're going to create history in Camelot!"

He swam as fast as he could, and she raced him, touching the other end of the pool before he did. They laughed and swam more races.

Lancelot was awed. Kate could wield a sword, and she could swim faster than heavily muscled Arthur. No dainty maiden. Merlin had tutored the knight about the fierce Picts in ancient Scotland, where the women fought alongside the men. Some were pagan priestesses who were revered as goddesses. Maybe Kate was one of these.

She and Arthur climbed out of the pool, gathered their clothes, and went inside.

"Almost too pretty," he'd heard her say. *That's how to describe a maiden, so was it a compliment?* Lancelot was proud of his physical strength and battle skills, but he didn't dwell on his appearance, maybe because there were few mirrors in his father's castle. And the attention the maidens paid him could be that he was titled and would someday inherit his father's castle and its vast estate. Knights were trained to be humble, not vain, but if Kate had complimented him, he was surprised at how good it made him feel.

*Strumming his lute, Lancelot* serenaded Arthur and Kate in the candlelit library. Geoffrey accompanied him on a dulcimer, a medieval stringed instrument played with wooden mallets. Merlin came into the room, drawn by the music. When the piece ended, he said, "That is one of my favorite tunes in Camelot."

"Did you write that?" Kate asked Lancelot.

"No, but I shalt playeth one I hath put pen to paper." In a rich baritone, Lancelot sang:

Oh pure heart

Oh unblemished soul

She sparkled as a sun-kissed sea

My lady est fairer than new snow

Oh pure heart, how doth I worship thee

Oh pure soul, how doth I adore thee

"That was lovely," Kate said.

"Thou art too gracious."

"Are you singing to a statue in a museum?" Geoffrey asked.

"To a woman I idolize ... in Camelot," Lancelot said.

"So, how does a guy get it on with a gal pure and frozen as the winter snow?"

This confused the knight. "Get it on?"

"You know," Geoffrey said. "Do the nasty." Then, reacting to the knight's dull stare, "Carnal engagement. Sex."

"Ideal love doth not allow for such a thing!"

"What do you think, guys?" Geoffrey asked Arthur and Kate. "Does Sir Lancelot have an unblemished soul?"

Kate knew what he was asking. "No comment." But it did make her wonder if Lancelot was a virgin.

"What do you think, Mr. King?"

Arthur, too, dodged the question. "He lives his code of honor."

"Well, my mind's a writhing snake pit of lust, and staying pure means too many cold showers to dampen the urge," Geoffrey said. "But I'm not just a sex fiend. Sally was the love of my life, and I wrote her a song."

Merlin came in just as Geoffrey began to sing about lovers who committed joint suicide. Buried in the same coffin, they sang to each other for eternity.

"Weird," Arthur muttered.

"That makes me more sad than happy," Kate said.

"But it's still a song about love." Geoffrey played the first few bars, then stopped. "Okay, campers, now you know the words, so sing along." He played a mellow introduction with his meaty hands on the mallets before he got to the melody. Arthur sang in his bass voice without enthusiasm. Merlin hummed and danced spryly but a little off the beat. Lancelot and Kate sang well and with pleasure, smiling as they harmonized. Lancelot's hand brushed against Kate's. He had made no conscious decision to touch her and wondered if his fingers had been possessed by a desire not his own. When the song ended, the knight said, "'Tis time for evening prayer," and left abruptly.

Merlin headed to his lab where he spent most of his time. Kate and Arthur stayed with Geoffrey, who played some of his favorite Broadway tunes, and as Arthur began to relax, he joined Geoffrey and Kate, singing with more enthusiasm.

*But Lancelot walked right by the chapel.* In his room, he sat on his bed and judged his hand as if it belonged to someone else. What was happening? How did it just reach out and touch Kate? He believed women were to be adored, not caressed. But what he felt for Kate had little to do with adoration, more like Geoffrey's swirling snake pit. The image of her near-naked body in the swimming pool haunted him. He shook his head to make it disappear. But like the touching hand, the memory had a separate will. He found the instant photo of Kate in a leather pouch on his belt. Serious Kate stared out at him. *What's happening? How can I have these feelings for an ideal woman?*

# CHAPTER 16



ARTHUR AND KATE GRABBED DAGGERS from the weapons room and headed outside for a walk in the tranquil, star-filled night.

As soon as the patio door closed behind them, Kate knew they'd made a terrible mistake. She sensed Morgan was dangerously near, and looking up, she saw a red-feathered and a black-feathered eagle diving out of the darkness. She grabbed Arthur's arm to pull him inside where he would be protected by Merlin's magical shield. But not in time. Dinosaur-sized red bird sank its talons into Arthur.

"No!" Kate shouted as Black-feather attacked her but retreated the moment she threatened it with her weapon. Arthur struggled to reach his dagger, but the bird immobilized his arms. Kate threw her dagger, and her blade sunk deep into Red-feather's wing. The eagle screeched a wild yet strangely human cry of pain. Then, without thinking of her safety, Kate jumped, grasping Arthur's legs to free him from the talons and pull him back to earth. He was horrified that she would die with him. "Let go!" he shouted.

The screech alerted Lancelot in his room. He grabbed his sword and sprinted to the terrace, waiving his sword futilely at the out-of-reach eagle. It surprised Kate that the warrior with ballet grace suddenly appeared unsure and clumsy.

The shrieks startled Merlin, who was engrossed in a virtual reality trip through outer space. He ripped off his goggles and hurried to the terrace, where the bird lifted Kate and Arthur. The wizard rubbed the blue sapphire in his pendant with one hand and pointed the other at Red-feathers, stunning it with sparking energy, causing its talons to lose their gripping power. Arthur and Kate tumbled to the terrace, stunned but not seriously hurt.

Geoffrey joined the fight but quickly realized the short-bladed paring knife he'd grabbed in the kitchen was a joke against the enormous birds. They flew up, outside the danger of Merlin's energy. Red-feathers circled, preparing to attack, but Black-feathers retreated even higher.

Merlin shape-changed into a pterodactyl, a winged dinosaur with an elongated beak filled with multiple rows of pointed teeth. It spread its bony, angled wings and flew up. Red-feathers was bright-eyed, thrilled to do battle.

The pterodactyl and the eagle sped toward each other. "I am all-powerful!" Red-feathers shrieked in Morgan's voice.

"Your need for revenge will bring only defeat," Merlin replied.

Screeches filled the night. The birds whirled and spun, then collided, wounding each other. Blood flowed from Red-feathers's wing and neck and trickled from a gash above the pterodactyl's eyes. Both beasts lost strength, and Red-feathers finally disengaged, fleeing into the darkness.

The pterodactyl descended and shape-changed into his human form. The wound on his head was not severe, and pressing a finger on it stopped the bleeding. The wizard summoned a pure white dove, ordering it to follow Morgan Le Fay and to report where she went. The bird soared up, keeping the eagle in sight.

Merlin flopped into an Adirondack chair near next to Kate and Lancelot, who tended to Arthur. Kate ripped off a strip of her shirttail to bind Arthur's wounds. "We better put some antiseptic on those punctures," she said. "You don't know what foul crap could be on the talons."

Arthur was much more concerned about Kate than the punctures in his shoulders. "Are you hurt?"

"I'm okay."

"There's no modern medicine here," Merlin said in a weak voice. "Is there honey in your kitchen, Geoffrey?"

"For sure. I use it to make medieval booze."

"Pour some on Arthur's and my wounds. That will act as an antiseptic."

They all headed into the kitchen, and Arthur realized Kate was limping. He put his arm around her shoulder. *She got hurt and didn't complain. Brilliant, loving, caring. Now brave and tough. Is there no end to the reasons I love her?*

Inside, where Kate daubed Arthur's and the wizard's wounds with honey, Merlin wondered why Lancelot had not been outside to protect Arthur. He saw a possible answer in how the knight kept glancing at Kate. Kate's magnetic personality appeared to be disrupting Lancelot's inner compass, and Merlin was concerned he might have lost his way.

*Weakened by the loss of her empowering blood, Morgan barely had the strength to fly back to her hotel suite in the city. Shape-changing into a ghostly pale human with dull red-barn hair, she bandaged her gashes. Then, too exhausted to make a rejuvenating potion, she collapsed into the king-sized bed she had demanded.*

*In the chapel, Lancelot prayed* on his knees, seeking forgiveness for neglecting his duty to the king. The knight shut his eyes but opened them when he heard something behind him. Merlin was sitting on a pew nearby. Strange. Lancelot had never seen the wizard in the chapel before.

"A closely fought battle tonight, don't you think, Sir Lancelot?"

"Thou saveth Kate and the king."

"Morgan was wounded, but she'll be back, and we must be ever alert to our duty."

*Was the wizard questioning my honor?*

Merlin smiled. "Congratulations on being named Minister of War, the second most trusted advisor to the king after the Hand. Do you know why Uther discharged Reginald?

"Rumors aboundeth it was about a title."

Merlin raised his arm, and a 3D image of Camelot's throne room appeared. This was similar to the vision the wizard had created earlier, only now, the Hand of the King's seat was occupied by the man Lancelot recognized as Reginald.

"He was the second most powerful man in the kingdom, but that did not quiet his ambitions." Merlin continued, "He desired to be named a duke with lands and income. But that would never happen because he wasn't the son of a noble family."

The wizard rotated the conjured image, and his intent became clear to Lancelot. Morgan was sitting on the king's throne, dripping with accessories of power. A jewel-laden crown sat jauntily on her head. She held a grapefruit-sized orb encrusted with gems in one hand and the jewel-bedecked royal gold wand called a scepter in the other.

"Reginald doth become Morgan's Hand! Traitor!" Lancelot declared.

Merlin fumbled through his many pockets until he found Lancelot's favorite photo of Kate. "Oh," Merlin said. "You dropped this on the terrace when you eventually joined the fight."

*I am disgraced, and my prayers for forgiveness are not answered.*

# CHAPTER 17

LANCELOT PATIENTLY TUTORED Arthur in Latin at the large library table where the toy soldiers were still set up while Kate examined book titles on the floor-to-ceiling shelves. She suddenly sensed Merlin was mentally communicating with her, and when she turned to the open door, he beckoned. "*Will you take a ride with me?*" she heard in her head.

She knew Arthur would be working with Lancelot for quite a while, but she hesitated. Merlin always had a hidden plan. "Ride? Into the future? The past? To get a quart of milk?"

"It will be an adventure, Kate," Merlin said aloud, knowing that would appeal to her. "We can defang Morgan."

*Me? I don't bring magic to the fight, and my sword skills are basic.* Kate looked over at the bulked-up warriors hunched over a book. "Wouldn't it be a good idea to bring the muscle?"

"They're busy right now," was his perplexing answer.

She would do anything to protect Arthur. She swallowed hard, then forced a brave smile. "Who wouldn't want to put 'defanging a sorceress' on their resume?"

Merlin nodded, and she read his mind. "*Arthur chose the right queen. Or was it she who picked the right king?*"

*The white scout dove gracefully banked* as it weaved through Midtown Manhattan skyscrapers. Below, Geoffrey followed it in his SUV with Merlin and Kate riding with him.

She realized there were neither edged weapons nor protective armor in the vehicle. If this was going to be a Wizard versus Sorceress smackdown, would the battle be all magic? May the most potent spell win. She'd asked how the fight would happen, but Merlin was more interested in discussing his science project. He was explaining that with information researched on the Internet and data from trial-and-error experiments, he was slowly building up the strength of the electric magnets in his lab.

"You're using the scientific method!" Kate said.

"Yes. There are limits to my powers, just as there are limits to what science can explain."

Kate sat back. So the wizard expanded his problem-solving ability by using a new way of thinking. Maybe she could increase her perception and analytical skills by not doubting her innate sensitivity and mind-reading capabilities.

Geoffrey wasn't horn-honking frustrated to be stuck in midnight Times Square traffic. When celebrities stopped using his services, his favorite time and place to drive for Uber was Forty-Second Street on Saturday night. He would miss picking up extravagant person-alities and overtipping drunks to photograph for his "Only-in-New York" album. The bouncy young ladies—whose idea of overdressing was short short-shorts and halter tops—striding along the sidewalks tonight made him frown instead of smile. There would be none of this hormonal exuberance in Camelot. The maidens he'd seen in tapestries were swaddled head to toe like mummies in museums.

The dove settled on the awning of a luxury hotel, and Geoffrey stopped across the street.

"Please drive around to the service entrance at the back?" Merlin asked.

Geoffrey idled near the open hotel loading dock, where workers accepted deliveries and put out the garbage in black plastic bags.

"Are you ready to face the enemy?" Merlin asked.

Whew! A knot of anxiety tightened in Kate's stomach, and exhaling, she showed him her empty hands. "No dagger. No sword. You must have a plan."

"You'll be fine," Merlin assured her.

"Well, if I'm not fine," she said to Geoffrey, "tell Arthur I love him."

"I'll deliver that message with a heavy heart."

The magician shape-changed into a king cobra. Kate's body started tingling, and she was disgusted to discover she had morphed into a giant snake. Even a tiny, venom-less snake made Kate squirm, but maybe Morgan feared them too, which would give snake-Kate an advantage.

Two six-foot cobras slithered out of the SUV, gliding by a white-haired night security guard who wore his baseball cap sideways like the teenagers. He looked up from his phone to see the snakes squeezing through an air-conditioning duct grate. The guard shook his head in disbelief. Naw! And returned to his video game.


*In her hotel suite, Morgan was deep* in a rejuvenating sleep. On the writing desk next to the hot plate, mini cauldron, and several leather pouches, Crow rested. Its species was always partially awake, unlike those pea-brained pigeons that did sleep. It immediately saw the cobras emerge from the air-conditioning vent. Crow shuddered. Much smaller snakes raided nests to eat crow eggs and fledglings; these gigantic serpents could swallow a full-grown crow in a heartbeat. It opened its beak to alert the sorceress, but a cobra spat, its venom freezing the bird into a feathery statue.

One rapidly crossed to the desk while the other headed for Morgan. The Merlin-cobra coiled and rose so its head was the same height as the desktop and grabbed the pouches in its mouth.

Kate-cobra extended her body until its head was very close to Morgan. Curled up with her knees raised to her chest, almost in a fetal position, the ashen sorceress appeared death-bed frail.

Ill or sick, she was still Arthur's mortal enemy and, therefore, her foe. Kate wondered if there was deadly venom in her fangs. One fatal bite on the exposed neck would end the battle. She's a sorceress, but not immortal? Can she die? Was this why Merlin had brought her? To do the dirty work? Morgan's breathing was labored and unusually loud. Her rhythmic sounds made Kate flash on a short story about a murderer who buried the victim under the floorboards of his own home. Increasingly tormented by guilt, the criminal hallucinated that the deceased's heart was still beating loudly, and the thumping eventually drove him insane. Would that be her fate if she killed Morgan? Forever haunted by her crime?

"I have her potion ingredients," Merlin-snake said. "We go now."

In the SUV's back seat, the cobras spread their hoods open and bared their fangs so Geoffrey could get an instant photo. "You boost all Morgan's bat wings and other disgusting potion junk?" he asked.

"Yes," the snake said in Merlin's voice, showing the pouches. "But it won't take her long to replace what I took and continue her vendetta."

"The wicked witch's lying up there half dead, and you've got her potion ingredients. Don't the folks in way-back-world know when they're beaten?" Geoffrey asked.

"They're usually dead before they give up," Merlin said.

"Sounds like the Wild West, only without cowboy hats," Geoffrey muttered as he pulled away from the hotel.

Merlin shape-changed slowly, and when he pointed his arm at the Kate-cobra, nothing happened. "Whoa, Merlin. What's going on? Get me out of this snakeskin!" The wizard closed his eyes to concentrate and rubbed his sapphire pendant. Finally, the snake morphed into Kate, and she shot Merlin a concerned look. "You ... your magic is okay?"

"I guess I just got a little tired."

Kate was puzzled but didn't push it. "Why didn't we kill Morgan?"

"Magicians' guiding principle is the same as modern doctors': first, do no harm. You've seen my magic to shape-change people and time travel. I can mimic magnetism but not implant that force into objects. But my capacity to do evil is minimal, and I cannot kill."

"But Morgan is trying to kill Arthur."

"After I taught her magic, she joined a coven of witches where she learned to override any restrictions I had implanted in her."

"Did you think that I could or would kill her?"

"Murder a defenseless woman who is your archenemy? Now we know."

Kate wondered if there was less moral restraint about violence and killing in ancient England. Would she have to become ruthless as queen? Maybe Camelot wasn't as ideal as Lancelot portrayed it.

"What did you learn about Morgan?" Merlin asked.

"That she has skin smooth as lab beaker glass. And she's not just a monster movie villainess. She's human."

"She has powers, but like humans, she has desires and emotions that diminish them."

"Such as?"

"She was the king's bastard daughter, and because he never acknowledged her existence, she grew to hate him. After he died, she transferred those feelings to her favored half-brother. So, it's not sufficient that Arthur dies. She must kill him herself for it to be satisfactory."

"Seeing Morgan up close wasn't a test of your ability to kill. But taking time to know your enemy can make you fight smarter and more efficiently. As Arthur, and probably you too, will discover in Camelot." Merlin patted Kate's shoulder tenderly. "We find out who we really are in the most extreme circumstances."

# CHAPTER 18

MORGAN CURSED MERLIN when she discovered her leather pouches were gone.

Wearing only her leopard-skin shawl, she grabbed a silver dinner knife from a room service tray and wildly stabbed the air. "You will die the death of a thousand cuts!" Then she spotted the crow with its beak half open. She touched the bird's head with a finger to free it from Merlin's curse. Nothing happened. *Oh man*, Crow thought. *I'm going to wind up on some poet's bookcase.*

The sorceress cupped both hands around Crow and mumbled a chant, animating it this time.

"I'm done, Crow! I could barely undo Merlin's curse on you. I will become a frail, pathetic human."

"As luck would have it, there is a pharmacy nearby. Rejuvenating potion, coming right up."

"Pharmacy?"

"I happen to enjoy Shakespeare and, in particular, the tragedy *Romeo and Juliet* set in medieval times. I think it might tickle your fancy because both young lovers die. In Camelot, a pharmacy would be called an apothecary shop."

*With Crow on her shoulder,* Morgan wound through the aisles of cosmetics, toys, and pain medications to the prescription counter in a neon-lit drugstore. With glasses so thick that the lenses enlarged her eyes, the pharmacist demanded, "Your script."

"These are the ingredients you will provide," Morgan commanded. Seeing a stylishly dressed customer with a pet crow instead of a little white dog didn't startle the cool New Yorker. But the customer's arrogant tone filled the eyes behind the lenses with hostility.

"I require frog toes, bat wings, dried laserwort, foxglove, and jimsonweed, three lizard livers, three drachms of newt tears, and a dozen forked snakes' tongues."

The pharmacist's stare got icier with each ingredient Morgan listed.

*Morgan, who prided herself* on rarely agonizing about anything, was worried. Her strength, intelligence, and deviousness could solve most problems. If not, there was always sorcery. As the pharmacist told her to get lost, Morgan didn't have the ingredients she needed to brew her needed potion. In her weakened condition, defeating Merlin and Arthur was impossible, as was time travel back to her throne in Camelot. And now she did fret.

Until Crow suggested they go to a botanica. Practitioners of Santeria, a mysterious faith similar to Voodoo, bought chicken bones used in fortune-telling, and herbs, ointments, and other enchantment ingredients there. Crow and a boat-tailed grackle from the Dominican

Republic had once gotten silly on exotic plants they found in the botanica's garbage.

Morgan rode uptown in a limousine with Crow perched on the roof and stopped in front of a three-story building, a garbage-strewn empty lot on one side and a one-story auto repair garage on the other. Elevated railroad tracks blocked much of the sunlight, and even in midday, dark shadows provided excellent cover for wanna-be murderers.

The thick-necked driver, big enough to be a professional wrestler, turned to Morgan with concern. "You sure you got the right address, lady?"

Morgan informed him that she never made mistakes and got out, wending her way to the entrance through aging parked cars customized with dents and graffiti. The door was locked, and Morgan was just about to use what magic she had left to blow it off its hinges when the lock buzzed open. Bottles, jars, and metal boxes crowded floor-to-ceiling shelves in no apparent order. Even Crow, who dined on dead animals, was spooked by the hundreds of eyeballs staring at them from a fish-tank-sized container. Dried plants hung so low from the ceiling Morgan had to brush them aside. Somewhere incense burned, and a rooster seemed to bow to Morgan. The sorceress sniffed the air, her head turning this way and that. Crow thought she looked like a dog investigating the scents in a new space. But a happy dog. Morgan was smiling.

The smooth-skinned, ageless proprietor emerged from behind a thick red velvet curtain. A colorful waterfall of glass beads and stone necklaces hung from her neck, and her head was wrapped in a turban decorated with colorful flowers, which Morgan knew were poisonous. The woman recognized Morgan's force at once and, taking the enormous cigar out of her mouth, said, with a black-toothed smile, "*Hola, hechicera.*"

Morgan sensed a mysticism in this woman she hadn't detected in any modern-day human. "Hello, priestess."

"Sí, *hermana*." The woman nodded. "You have found me."

She led Morgan and Crow down a dark hall to a heavy metal door. A large key that looked like it could open an ancient castle dungeon hung from her belt, and the lock in the heavy door made a clunk when it opened. They entered a room lit with blacklights where plant leaves, flower blossoms, and jars of ingredients glowed eerily. From the relief on her face, Crow knew Morgan had found what she needed.

"Double double trouble trouble for the wiz and cutie-pie," Crow cawed.

*Morgan smoked a fat cigar* in the back of the limo as she and Crow rode downtown. Next to her was a colorful plastic shopping bag with all her needed ingredients. "Where does Arthur's maiden live?"

"Close," Crow cawed. "Her building's on a crosstown street four blocks away. Number 334."

The sorceress pulled some plants from the bag and chewed on them until her hair turned a deeper shade of red. "We'll see if any of her possessions indicate any vulnerability."

"What could be more fun than that!"

Morgan ordered the driver to turn left, stop in front of 334, and wait for them. The sorceress's plants restored enough of her powers that when she got out of the limo, she was able to shape-change into a bright yellow oriole. She and Crow flew to Kate's open bedroom window, hopped through, and alighted on the dresser next to several framed photographs. One showed teenage Kate jumping a horse over a high fence. "She's fair for a peasant," Morgan-bird said.

Morgan shape-changed into human form, opened the closet, and pulled out blouses and jeans. "Thrift shop or sale bin. Not suitable for the queen," Crow advised. Morgan then checked the dresser's top drawer and found a Columbia University student ID. "What's this?"

"A magic card that lets smart kids become smarter."

"And more powerful."

"No one is as powerful as Your Royal Invincible-ness." Crow heard something and flew to the window. Below, Rita was sitting on the fire escape, talking on her phone. "You got a bed for me in your cult?"

Morgan joined Crow, and they heard Kate's voice on Rita's phone ask, "What up, girl?"

"I just got the tuition bill from my community college. It ain't like 75,000 grand at your stuck-up university, but it's big money to me. I showed the bill to the 'rents, and what do I hear? Nothing is left in the college fund for the child who isn't muchacho. Adored son got it all and graduated without a nickel of loans. I'm no scholarship genius like you, so I gotta borrow three G's just for my first semester."

"That sucks."

"Big time."

Rita's phone buzzed, and she looked at the incoming number. "Gotta take a call from my EMS shit boss. Stay in touch unless they cut your head off or something."

Morgan stared at Rita for a long time. "Her favored older brother gets the money," she muttered. "She's probably smarter than him too."

"Like Morgan Le Fay is more brilliant that dunderhead Arthur," Crow said with a hint of sarcasm Morgan missed.

"It's not FAIR!" Morgan rubbed her finger over the ID photo, transforming Kate's image into Rita's. "Leave this on that girl's windowsill."

"Your wish is my command, Your Royal Empathyness."

"Women have been beaten down for thousands of years." Morgan raised her fist in anger. "I'm going to change that!"

*Vapors bubbled up from the potion* cooking on Morgan's hot plate. Next to it was the empty plastic bag from the botanica. She lifted the mini cauldron and gulped more of the boiling liquid. Reclining on a sofa in a slinky nightgown as her hair turned hostile red, she watched a TV show about shotguns.

The TV instructor was blasting wooden targets that exploded into a circle of splinters. "Magnificent!" Morgan declared. "What destruction comes out of that vengeance stick!"

*Vengeance stick?* "Oh, the shotgun. No magic. Pull the trigger and a bullet flies out of the metal barrel and that thing that's no bigger than your thumb can cause a world of hurt. You use it on a person and they'll swim with the fishes."

"You insult my intelligence by using expressions the queen does not know."

"Does the queen disdain plain language? Most certainly. 'Swims with the fishes' is a figure of speech that describes someone who has been killed and then dumped into a river or ocean."

"Yes, beautiful poetry, Crow. Now, forget edged weapons. Take me to the royal gunsmith!"

"Democracy's shortcomings again, Your Royal Assassin-ess. There are gun stores everywhere. Americans have the constitutional right to defend themselves."

"I see no wild beasts hunting flesh on the city streets. No barbarian marauders or untamed Picts looting and raping. What do they defend themselves against?"

Crow shrugged. "Fear, I guess."

"Dumb. These bullet things can't kill fear. But they can ... as the poet rhapsodizes, make a dishwasher 'swim with the fishes.'"

*In sword practice, Arthur gripped* his weapon in a defensive posture as he focused on Merlin, holding a wooden bow with an arrow knocked in the taut string. The young king didn't notice Kate and Lancelot walking through the field behind him.

Lancelot had apprised the wizard of Arthur's excellent

fundamental sword-fighting skills. So now the wizard would train Arthur to become more than a technical fighter. "Trusting your instincts will liberate you from thinking about your parry or a step across. Doubt will no longer restrain you."

This made sense to Arthur. His karate sensei had started to train him to have a "free mind," uncluttered by preconceived notions of fighting. Merlin fired an arrow, and lacking a helmet or padded jacket's protection, Arthur deflected it with his sword, along with other arrows the wizard rapidly fired. With each arrow, the young warrior sensed his vision becoming sharper, his motor skills quicker. He began to feel the "runner's high" he experienced on long training runs in New York when the endorphin chemicals in his brain triggered elation.

Now, the arrows flying at him exploded into snakes baring fangs. The serpents attacked Arthur from all sides. Wielding his sword in one hand and his dagger in the other, Arthur sliced the heads off the creatures until the remaining ones retreated. They coiled around each other to morph into an eight-foot-tall woman draped in animal hides swinging a bloodstained axe. It swept back and forth with such speed that Arthur heard a "swish" each time. Holding his sword with both hands, Arthur used all his power to sever the axe's blade from the handle as it arced by. Then the defenseless giant morphed into Merlin.

Arthur thrust his sword into the earth and rested on it, exhausted, head-bowed, panting. It took a moment to catch his breath.

"You must be ready for the unexpected in combat," Merlin said.

*The sun shone through the dense,* leafy canopy above the woodland path, creating areas of bright light and deep shadow.

Lancelot had told Kate there was a perfect maiden in Camelot whom he idolized, and he wanted to write her a poem. "I hath no words to express the love I feel. I am like a blasphemer whose tongue hath been cut."

"This woman can't be ideal. No woman or man can be."

"She hath no flaws," Lancelot said, locking his eyes on Kate. "She est purest of all."

Why did she think for one moment that this woman he was talking about was anyone but her? Lancelot's sidelong glances, love songs, and knightly flowery flirting all pointed to this moment. *But how can he think I'm a pure, ideal woman? Does he think my armpits don't stink?*

She did admire the poetic way Lancelot described life in Camelot and realized that beneath the chain mail, he had an appealing sensitivity. Lancelot was sometimes so stiff, and his sincerity so forced, it appeared he was reading out of a knight's trite handbook. He was almost childlike in his unquestioned beliefs. This guileless knight was the pure one, and she connected with him when they sang with Geoffrey.

Lancelot didn't confess his love for her, and his Code of Chivalry protects him from acting on his yearnings for his king's and best friend's woman. *My warm affection for him is like that for a brother I never had. But what if these feelings turned hot?*

*The only time Arthur nodded off* before Kate was after making vigorous love. He lay on his back with her head resting on his shoulder in their king-sized bed. His eyes were closed, and his breathing had the soft rhythm of sleep. She didn't move a muscle until she was sure he was asleep. Then, slipping out of bed, she quietly dressed and went out.

*The wizard wasn't in his work lab,* but the doors leading outside were open. Kate dodged through the jumble of gadgets and toys to find Merlin peering through a telescope on the lawn. He looked up as she approached. "It's such a waste of time to sleep in this world. There's too much exciting magic to discover. Come look, Kate!" he beckoned. "Binary stars!"

She shook her head.

"No interest in the heavens?" Merlin asked.

"Not tonight."

For Kate, stars were abstract and represented something so vast and timeless that the heavens were almost impossible to comprehend. What was very real on planet Earth were her confused emotions. She'd never loved anyone with the intensity that she loved Arthur. But what was this feeling she had for Lancelot?

"Can I ask you a personal question, Merlin?"

"All questions are personal, aren't they?"

She hoped darkness made revelations easier. "Were you ever in love?"

"Yes. With beautiful Clarissa, who helped me bring baby Arthur into the present. She liked it here and broke my heart when she did not return to Camelot."

"Has any other woman attracted you?"

"Magic and discovery became the objects of my affection, and I did not have the time or commitment a relationship requires." He paused, and she sensed the image of Clarissa might have jumped into his consciousness. "But when I returned to the present, she began haunting me again," he said with a sad smile. "Is there another man haunting you? Is your heart a crowded place?"

She didn't know why, but she trusted Merlin would not reveal her divided love to Arthur. "I'm fascinated by Lancelot."

"Love maybe?"

"I don't think so. It's just that he's such a compelling mixture of ideals and animal aggression. A brutal warrior who writes poetic love songs."

Merlin peered through the telescope for a long moment. "Being loved as the person you are may be more meaningful and enduring than being worshipped as an ideal."

He was steering her toward Arthur. She hoped Lancelot loved the idea of loving her, more than loving her as a person. She wanted to be with Arthur for the rest of her life. But she wondered, would there come a time when she was in the arms of her future husband that behind her closed eyes, she'd dream of being with warrior poet?

Pointing to the heavens, Merlin said, "The binary stars are brothers. But their closeness eventually gets them tangled in each other's gravitational field and they crash together, creating a vast cosmic explosion that destroys them both."

"Tonight?"

He chuckled. "It will happen, but maybe not for a million years."

With the two shining stars in Kate's universe, the possibility of an explosion might not take quite that long.

# CHAPTER 19

SITTING AT A MASSIVE DESK in the library, Kate and
Arthur studied a leather-bound, handwritten, illustrated text. Geoffrey
ambled in, wearing his apron and carrying a mug of ale. "Yikes! I'm
having a nightmare that I'm back in study hall hell. What's that fat
doorstop of a book?"

"This is the Latin textbook Merlin used to tutor Lancelot," Kate
said. "Priscian's *Institutiones grammaticae. From Roman times, a thousand years before Camelot even existed.*"

"*I'm on permanent summer vacation. No books, especially thick books.
Come on. The wiz wants to show us something. Where's the big guy?*"

"*Outside standing guard,*" Arthur said.

"*He's all duty duty duty. I hope some knights in the old days like
to party.*"

Geoffrey rounded up Lancelot, and all went into Merlin's lab,
where he had used his 3D printer to create a four-foot-tall model of

the Art Deco Chrysler Building. On each of its four corners, not far below the building's needle-shaped peak, were stylized sculptures of eagles' heads.

Lancelot moved to the opposite side of the model from Kate to prevent his rogue hands from seeking her out. Merlin put a finger on one of the eagle heads. "We'll launch from here."

"When you say 'launch,' that makes me think you have a rocket ship or time machine," Geoffrey said.

"We will dive off to time travel."

"Those birds are what, sixty floors above the sidewalk? So I see two distinct outcomes," Geoffrey said. "Becoming a grease spot on Forty-Second Street and getting my picture in the tabloids, which I'll be too dead to appreciate. Or better, winding up in Camelot surrounded by adoring barmaids." He laughed nervously.

"Is the king ready?" Merlin asked Lancelot.

Lancelot nodded at Arthur. "He hath the heart of a warrior and now the skill of a knight."

"That is good because the day after tomorrow, a comet passes with the first rays of dawn, and we'll ride it to Camelot."

*Merlin explained to Kate and Arthur* that no modern-day material like nylon or plastic would survive time travel. Besides Kate's locket on its gold chain, the linen clothes they now wore and the chain-mail armor made of forged steel would be the only possessions they could bring. Kate laid out her worldly belongings on one side of their bed. She'd arrived at the horse farm with only what she'd had on: jeans, a shirt, underwear, and cell phone. She held up her bra. "Do they have these in Camelot?"

"I flunked the course on medieval lady's underwear."

*Arthur's definitely developing a king-like intolerance for foolishness but still has a sense of humor. Thank goodness,* she thought.

"Pretty meager pickings," Kate said. "I read that the last queen of England traveled with forty suitcases."

"No worries. Merlin tells me my father and mother left many royal garments at Castle Camelot."

Next to hers, he placed two pairs of shorts, three T-shirts, underwear, and his phone.

"Okay, what do you wish you could bring?" Kate asked.

He picked up Ulysses Grant's autobiography from the side table and leafed through the pages. "There are excellent examples of how to lead an army and govern. And I'd bring my karate medal that the police took when they arrested me."

"I didn't think you were into trophies."

"When I got kicked out of my foster home and the shelters, I left everything behind: clothes, shoes, toothbrush ... I wanted a fresh start wherever I got sent without the stench of the shitholes I was leaving." He placed the book on the bed. "All I took were my books and my award."

Arthur had told Kate little about his childhood. He'd never talked about living on the streets, and only offered bits and pieces about the youth shelters and his foster parents. But she sensed there were abuses and humiliations at every place based on his bottled-up rage. That he focused on successful events rather than defeats was one of the many reasons she admired the former dishwasher. "Are you leaving the stink of the present time behind?"

"I hadn't thought of it like that, but yeah, that sounds right."

"How about people?"

He closed his eyes. "I'll miss Nikos and Tiny Toni. I know they'd be super happy about what's happened to me." Then, eyes open, he looked around the room. "I'll miss this place. It's the only school where the rules and lessons have all made sense. Merlin and Lancelot don't think I'm a mentally challenged punk who only knows how to confront the world with his fists." He rubbed the back of Kate's hand. "What'll you miss?"

"Like you, I don't think I'll miss things." Kate dumped her keys, MetroCard, and other debris from her backpack onto the bed. "I'm sad I'll never see Rita become a doctor or my old babysitter Valerie get her associate's degree from night college." She picked up a color photo of her mother and grandmother and fingered the locket hanging around her neck. "I'll miss Grandmom." She then turned over her internship chemistry lab ID so the photo was face down. "And science."

"You'll be leading the citizens out of the darkness," Arthur said in his best positive voice.

"If they don't burn me at the stake for being a witch."

Arthur wrapped his arms around Kate from behind. "Never in my kingdom."

She titled her head back until it was next to his.

*As Lancelot stood guard outside the mansion,* his vigilance was disturbed by the silhouette of Kate and Arthur through their bedroom window. A collision of envy and disapproval made the knight turn away to face a bloodred crescent moon rising above the treetops. As a young squire, he'd learned from Merlin how the Picts believed the moon had mysterious power. Most of their rituals took place in its ghostly light, led by the priestesses, who were worshipped as goddesses. But then Lancelot's religious tutors had badgered any curiosity about the pagan ceremonies out of him. Instead, they instilled devotion, self-discipline, and celibacy.

Lancelot again looked at the couple embracing. Was Kate a moon goddess? He didn't think she'd bewitched him, but her radiant presence made him lightheaded and his heart race. His desire for her untethered him from his faith. Had he fallen into a river where he couldn't swim out of the rushing current? Or had he jumped in without thinking of the consequences? In any case, he could not, would not, deny his love for her a moment longer.

*Geoffrey ate a vast mouthful of homemade pâté* and washed it down with a big swig of ale just as Lancelot strode into the kitchen.

"Where's the battle, big guy?" Geoffrey asked.

"I goeth to Kate."

"Kate has chosen her man, and as we are chatting here, she might even be tangled up between the sheets with the king. Back in Camelotville, I'll bet plenty of maidens are eager to be idolized by a hunky knight with his own castle." He took a drink. "And yours truly hopes that more than a few maidens are eager for something less spiritual."

"But I must declare my true love for her!"

"What is it with you and this truth thing?" Geoffrey gobbled more pâté. "Kate's beautiful and sexy without trying, which a lady can only be if she's sexy without trying. She's really smart if you happen to like that in a girl. She's considerate and caring. Arthur loves Kate. I love Kate. Merlin loves Kate. And now you love Kate. But there's a 'but.'"

Geoffrey put down his drink and illustrated his words with his hands. "Arthur's the king, and from what I hear about the seventh century, fooling around with the king's woman will get your big head cut off ... and your little head too, probably in reverse order. Ouch."

Lancelot slumped into a chair. In his time, he'd never associate with a lowly chef, particularly one with an insolent tongue and bawdy thoughts, but Geoffrey had made the knight reflect. His love could indeed make him disloyal to the king. "She invadeth my thoughts day and night. I knoweth that maketh me weak on the battlefield, yet I don't want to make them go away."

Geoffrey shook his head. *Is this guy hopeless or what?* He opened the door to a pantry where he'd set up a still and brought out a large earthen jug filled with a clear liquid. "Drink this with a lady, and you'll make an intimate friend. Drink it and laugh too hard at unfunny jokes. And this applies to you: drink it to forget. Drink up and forget Kate. You medieval dudes aren't the only ones with magic potions."

"Magic?"

"Absolutely."

Lancelot smelled the liquid, took three long gulps, and gasped as the alcohol seared his throat.

Geoffrey's belly shook as he laughed. "My man!"

*The chef and the knight floated* on inflatable rafts in the pool. The chef's clothes were soaked, and the weight of Lancelot's heavy chain mail just about sank him. Geoffrey took a drink from the jug and passed it to Lancelot, who poured it out.

"Hey!" Geoffrey yelled.

"I swore an oath of temperance," the knight slurred.

"Well, you're already so drunk you can hardly stand up. One oath down. How many more can we violate tonight?"

Lancelot's mind was reeling. Geoffrey's potion was filled with more demons than forgetfulness. His hunger for Kate only intensified. "In Camelot, I prayed devoutly, and God vanquished my urges."

Geoffrey hummed the tune from the Rolling Stones' song "Brown Sugar."

"Now, my prayers goeth unanswered. God doth hear me not."

"There's nothing wrong with urges. We all have them. And the good news is, maidens do too. Maybe not always on our schedule, but they do."

"Such desires make us no better than the godless beasts in the field."

"Your god wouldn't have given us the equipment if he didn't want us to use it. But you don't want to despoil any fair maiden, and you don't know how to make the urges disappear. Maybe that's why you're so tightly wound." Geoffrey paddled close to the knight and whispered theatrically, "Let me tell you about the joys of masturbation."

"She loveth me the most. I seeth how she admires me. No knight hath more valor or power than I. My sword doth defeat any man."

"Whoa, Sir Shit-faced. Time for you to sleep off those dangerous vodka thoughts."

*Kate was jumping on a bed.* Her cheeks were glowing from inner heat. Eyes bright. Hair flowing free. Her mouth was slightly open, with an openhearted smile. Art was jumping too. Both he and Kate still wore only the underwear they had on in the pool. They clasped hands, pulling each other close. Close enough to catch a fleeting kiss at the top of their bounces, and on the way down, Kate howled with glee.

The wooden feet of the bed slammed noisily against the floor.

*Lancelot lay naked on his bed* in the room next door, the world spinning around him. He opened his eyes, which steadied the reeling walls and ceiling a bit. But the alcohol had blurred his vision so that every object was doubled. He sat up and stared into a mirror, horrified by the sight of his drunken self and his ghost twin, a slack-jawed knight without substance.

*What was that woman's scream and awful pounding noise coming from Arthur's bedroom?*

To Lancelot's drunken brain, he was convinced Kate must be in pain. *Her life is threatened!* He could regain at least part of his self-respect by saving her.

He stood unsteadily, and when he leaned down to pick up his sword, he tumbled into the small altar he had set up, knocking the cross onto the floor. He grasped his weapon, braced himself against a wall to get up, then staggered out.

Just as he flung open the door, Arthur and Kate tumbled together in a way that she fell first and Arthur landed on top of her. They were both laughing so hard, tears filled their eyes. Misunderstanding, the knight brandished his sword above his head and slurred, "I shalt save thee from thy beast!"

Arthur rolled off her and pushed Kate out of the weapon's reach. "Lancelot, put that sword down!" Arthur commanded.

The knight hesitated, allowing Arthur to jump up and use a backhanded karate chop to knock the weapon out of Lancelot's grip. As the sword dropped, it sliced Arthur's shoulder. Too pumped with adrenaline to feel pain, Arthur grappled with Lancelot. The mighty knight's eyes went wide with horror when he saw blood seeping out of the wound. Immediately he stopped struggling. "I hath wounded my king. I hath wounded my brother." Tears streamed down his face.

Kate came around the bed to inspect the wound. "You okay?"

Arthur nodded and looked at the gash. "Not life-threatening. Sorry I had to push you out of the way."

"Talk about ruining our moment." She grinned. "Lancelot must have read the knights' instruction manual wrong. He is supposed to save damsels in distress, not put them in distress."

They pulled Lancelot to his feet and he mumbled, "I am disgraced in front of my king and the woman I doth worship." Then, he staggered into his bedroom and collapsed to the floor.

Arthur and Kate went into the adjoining bathroom, where he sat on the edge of the deep marble tub. After gently cleaning the wound, she pressed a rag on it to stop the bleeding. "That was really spooky. He really was going to kill you, Arthur."

"Drunks do some crazy shit. But in a million years, I would never have suspected Lancelot would let himself get so out of control."

Kate had a front-row seat to witness the emergence of the man she'd always sensed was buried inside her proud dishwasher. She held his hands and realized they were no longer chapped from being immersed in hot, soapy water. "You were so coolheaded and fearless. So decisive, Arthur. I—"

"Did you know he loves you?" Arthur interrupted.

Kate had hoped her feelings for Lancelot and his idolization of her would be their secret. But drunkenness had revealed the truth. "He never declared it, but I sensed he did."

Arthur had always feared Kate would stop loving him because her orbit was much greater than his. However, he hadn't imagined she would ever fall for someone else. He faced her directly to see if her eyes revealed betrayal. "Do you love him?"

She momentarily considered lying, but she knew that would ultimately cause terminal damage. "I think Lancelot writes lovely songs, and I admire his character and how he lives with such clarity of purpose and ideals." Kate paused. "Although after his escapade tonight, I'm questioning my judgment. So, if what I feel for him is love, it's love for a friend or brother, not a lover." She cupped Arthur's face in her hands with a tenderness that she hoped would remove any doubt. "It's you I love and want to be my life-long husband and lusty partner."

Her promise only partially assured him. *Will there be a time when she and Lancelot do act on their love?*

*In his room, Lancelot kneeled unsteadily.* He'd violated temperance and loyalty to the king. The Code of Chivalry required he endure the punishment of degradation. His was still seeing double, and the room was unsteady, but the images in his mind were as sharp as if lit by bright sunlight. He was kneeling on the cold stones of a Camelot courtyard surrounded by knights wearing chain mail and insignia-adorned tunics. Lancelot recognized his brothers and companions as they ceremoniously smashed his shield into pieces. Next, one by one, they hit the flat part of Lancelot's sword on his head until the blade broke. Then Lancelot had to climb into an open casket, which the knights dragged to a church. There, a priest held a burial mass. Lancelot of the Lake was no longer "sir." The young knight was dead forever!

He had one hope of redemption. He would seclude himself in an ancient monastery where lust could not overpower his faith, and liquor could not wash away his honor. Wrapping a blanket around himself, he stumbled out of his bedroom.

*Geoffrey stuck his head into* the bedroom where Kate and Arthur sat on the tub's edge in their underwear, and she continued to press a cloth on his wound. Blood was seeping through the fabric. The chef nodded his head with a leering grin. "What up? Lancelot lurched out of the house with only a blanket over him," Geoffrey said too deliberately, trying unsuccessfully to disguise his drunkenness.

"He barged in on us," Kate said.

"Phew. Nothing more disappointing than *coitus interruptus*," Geoffrey mumbled and picked up Lancelot's sword from the floor. "Especially if the interrupter is armed and dangerous."

"We did have a little tussle."

"I'll say. You don't get a cut that bleeds through a bandage kissing too hard. You going to survive?"

"I'll live to fight another day."

"That's the warrior spirit that us peons like to see in our king," Geoffrey said, bracing himself on the doorframe.

*The drunken knight stumbled* along a dark country road and stopped at a four-corner crossroad. Which way to go? He turned to the left into a gentle breeze. This couldn't be the right way, so he turned around and, with the wind at his back, lurched toward some glowing lights.

Lancelot had lost all sense of time and didn't know how long he had been wandering along country roads until he stumbled into the parking lot of an all-night diner on bruised and bleeding bare feet. A man with close-cropped white hair came out of the restaurant with a large cup of coffee, snapping his fingers to a tune he heard in his head.

"Where ...?" Lancelot mumbled.

The man stopped by the garbage truck he was about to get into and laughed. "Musta been some party."

"Chrys Building."

"Chrysler Building? What about it?"

"I hath to go there to travel back to Camelot."

"Man, you're gin drunk." The driver pointed in the opposite direction Lancelot had been going. "The city's that way."

When Lancelot turned around, he almost lost his balance.

"Okay, you'll never get there by walking." The driver pointed to his truck. "I got a load of demo to pick up at a construction site not far from Lex and Forty-Second. Hop in."

Lancelot staggered to the passenger side door, climbed up into the cab, and tumbled onto the seat. The driver chuckled. "I got three guesses. First, your woman tossed you out when you came home stinking drunk. Second, you were with someone else's woman and had to jump out the bedroom window when her man came home. And my best shot, your boss decreed no more working at home and to get your ass into the office. No matter how you're dressed."

# CHAPTER 20

MORGAN WAS ADMIRING HERSELF in the full-length mirror in a gun shop on Madison Avenue that could pass for a movie set of a swanky shotgun store for millionaires. The walls were lined with handmade Italian guns that glistened like gems. She looked more city-stylish than hunter in her khaki safari jacket, broadbrimmed slouch sun hat, and supple leather thigh-high boots that she grabbed from a rack up front."

"You look positively Hemingwayesque, Your Royal Safari-ness," Crow cawed, as it sat on Morgan's shoulder.

"Do not insult me that I resemble that lowly nine-fingered boot-maker Hemingway from Yorkshire!" Morgan said.

"Our Hemingway was a great hunter and almost as clever and daring as the queen. Although he would have had a problem with a strong woman like you."

"Why do I want to behead you and knight you at the same time?"

"May I be so bold as to suggest your Royal Brilliant-ness enjoys my wit and dim view of humanity."

"Whatever."

Very few things in modern New York City made Crow nervous, but it did fear shotguns. Sure, even a vigilant bird could be run over by a careening taxi or a savage garbage truck. But there were few natural enemies in the streets. Not many owls, hawks, or even eagles flying around Midtown. However, humans used guns to kill crows for sport, and Crow seldom ventured out to the country. So it had tried to steer Morgan to a sports store where they sold competition-grade bows and arrows. In the queen's world, only peasants served as archers in the medieval armies.

"Bring me a vengeance stick," Morgan commanded the handsome salesman. *Maybe an Ivy Leaguer who was taking a year off or who failed French One twice?* Crow judged. His eyes went wide. "I beg your pardon, madam?"

"A gun. A shotgun."

"12, 16, 20 gauge? And any particular price range?"

"Anything that goes well with this outfit?"

The young man smiled and brought her a gun where the wood on the stock was as deeply grained as marble. The metal on the sides near the trigger were etched with complex designs of birds in flight. In *Vogue Italia*, Crow had seen guns like these used by billionaires hunting on their estates in Tuscany. Morgan was not satisfied. "Bring me something gold."

The salesman flashed a condescending smile, and Crow guessed what he was thinking: New Money. "Of course, madam."

The walls of the store were dark, polished panels. He pressed his hand on the wood and a hidden door opened. He went in and returned with a weapon that had two barrels, one atop the other. To Crow, it was no way close to being as elegant as the other weapons. But it was golden.

Morgan yanked it out of the salesman's hand and posed with it in the mirror. "Royally lethal!"

"In America, we don't care much about royalty. But we do know about deadly. And you're holding an armful of lethal."

She pulled the trigger and nothing happened. "It's broken!"

"No madam. It's not loaded with ammunition." He opened a box of shells and pulled out two to show her.

Morgan grabbed the shells, inserted them into the weapon, pointed it at a manikin and fired twice. The roar of the gunshots in the enclosed space was deafening. Every salesperson and customer dove for the floor.

"Come Crow," she commanded, and grabbing the box of shells, she marched out of the store with the bird on her shoulder. On the avenue, pedestrians fled when they saw a woman with a menacing-looking shotgun. A police car roared up, but before the officers could jump out, Morgan shape-changed into a hawk and grasped the weapon with its talons. "Follow me," she ordered, and flew upward.

"Only if Your Royal Crow Hunter-ness controls your hawk DNA that needs to kill me," Crow cawed.

"Get your tailfeather up here now or I'll use this vengeance stick on you."


At *the horse farm mansion*, Arthur and Kate's search for drunken, bedsheet-covered Lancelot had been unsuccessful, and they were about to abandon caution to go outside to look for him when Merlin blocked their way. "You must stay inside the protective shield."

"What if Lancelot is passed out in the stable or has fallen face down in a mud puddle?" Arthur asked.

A pigeon appeared at the window, and the wizard let it in. "We'll know in a moment," Merlin said.

The bird startled Kate when it landed on her shoulder, cooing. Then she smiled. "Hello little friend."

"What's it telling you?"

"How could I understand a bird's cooing?"

"When you open your mind, you will."

Merlin stretched out his arm, and the pigeon fluttered over to coo in the wizard's ear. "I sent a flock to locate Lancelot, and my sharp-eyed friend here found the knight crumpled on the sidewalk at the base of the Chrysler Building. I'll get him up to the sixty-first floor, where we'll launch to Camelot. I scouted the area earlier and the entire floor is unoccupied. For some reason, there's a small Buddhist shrine there and that will protect him from Morgan."

Merlin opened the patio door. "Ah … Morgan est nigh," momentarily falling back into his Old England way of speaking. "Stay inside. I'll return to escort you to the past."

Merlin shape-changed into a snowy owl and soared upward.

*Hiding in bushes not far from the mansion,* Morgan smirked as she watched the owl disappear into the distance through her binoculars. She pumped a shell into the firing chamber on her shotgun with a metallic clunk that made Crow shudder. To keep itself where Morgan couldn't shoot at it if she was angered by something Crow did or said, the bird perched on her shoulder, near her head. "Arthur's sword will be useless against your vengeance stick," Crow said, its voice shaking with anxiety.

"Exploiting inequality is how history is made, Crow."

Morgan strode to the mansion, and when she put a hand on a doorknob, a powerful electrical shock staggered her backward, slime covering her hand. *What?* She looked up and saw the sunlight shimmering off a soapy, bubble-like film surrounding the entire building. She stuck the shotgun's barrel into the film, sending an electric shock through the metal gun into Morgan's arm, forcing her to drop the weapon. "Bat scat! A protective spell."

Morgan pulled a vial from her vest pocket and gulped down the glowing green liquid. Her hair turned blazing red, and confident of her increased power, she punched her fist into the bubble. Again, an electrical shock staggered her backward.

"Merlin!!!" she cursed.

*On the city sidewalk*, Lancelot was slumped beside an unshaven man with tangled, unwashed hair. No longer stinking drunk, cold sobriety punctured Lancelot's delusions of returning to Camelot. He felt imprisoned in this world where his strengths made him weak, and his weaknesses grew strong. His only wish was that Arthur had killed him in their bedroom fight.

It was late. A few men and women hustled toward the nearby Grand Central Terminal to catch the last commuter train home. None of the businessmen striding to work gave a second glance at a disheveled white-haired drunk and a half-naked younger man slouched on the sidewalk. But a few women did sneak a peek at the heavily muscled hunk only partially covered by a blanket.

The disheveled man passed a bottle in a paper bag to Lancelot, who refused, just as an owl landed on the sidewalk. "We're going home, Lancelot," the bird said in Merlin's voice.

"Save me from this loathsome time!"

The bird extended its wing, touching Lancelot's shoulder. Disheveled watched with incredulous eyes as Lancelot morphed into a red-tailed hawk and flew with the owl up to the sixty-first floor, where they perched on an ornamental Art Deco eagle's head.

On the sidewalk, Disheveled eyed the paper bag, then theatrically poured out the remaining demon liquor.

*Inside the mansion garage*, Geoffrey stuffed armor into a large leather duffel bag and put it in the trunk of his SUV.

Arthur and Kate were in the back seat, with Merlin up front. Geoffrey climbed behind the wheel, pulled out, and abruptly stopped. The wizard pointed his arm through the open window until the shimmering film surrounding the building disappeared.

Crouched in the shadows behind the mansion, Morgan said, "Something just happened, Crow." Looking at the building from her hiding place, the sorceress could not see or sense Merlin's protective bubble. She grabbed the shotgun, charged to the mansion, and warily touched a door handle. Nothing! Flinging open the entrance to Merlin's lab, she saw the Chrysler Building model and instantly understood where Merlin was taking Arthur. "Tomorrow, at first light, there's a celestial event, Crow!"

Crow nodded. *She's going to cancel their flight.*

In the driveway, Merlin again pointed his arm, and the shimmering bubble reappeared around the mansion. Then the SUV accelerated away.

When she heard the tires crunch on the driveway gravel, Morgan realized Merlin and Arthur might still be nearby. She rushed to open the front door and was stunned by a power jolt of electricity when she touched the inside knob. Again, she cursed Merlin.

*She dresses more fashionably than Merlin, but her eagerness to shoot her brother made her forget how sly the bumbling old wizard was, Crow thought.* "How about the artillery?" it asked.

"The what?"

"The vengeance stick, as you so poetically describe your shotgun. Blast your way out. A twenty-first century solution to a seventh-century spell."

Morgan pointed her gun at the door and fired. Wood splintered and sparks cascaded off the hinges as the door fell forward. Morgan stepped through the opening and fired again, puncturing a hole in the shimmering bubble. She jumped through. "I will definitely knight you In Camelot, Crow!"

*Sir Crow. Sounds like a rap star. Way cool.*

The SUV was turning onto the country road. Morgan shot at it until there was no more ammunition, but the vehicle was beyond the bullets' range. The SUV disappeared into the countryside, and the only sounds were the rustling of leaves in a gentle breeze and chirping cicadas.

The sorceress was always in motion, or some part of her was. A foot tapping. Shoulders rolling. Now she stood so still for so long, Crow thought she might be in a trance. Finally, Morgan muttered, "Of course, you dunce!" Her lips curled into a smile and she lovingly propped her weapon against a mansion pillar. From her leather pouch tied to her belt, she brought out a perfume bottle. She rocked back and forth to some inner music as she sprayed herself from head to toe. "Wars are won on the battlefield and lost in the bedroom. Do you smell silphium, Crow?"

That discount-store perfume masked Morgan Le Fey's distinctive sweet, sulfurous aroma of the herb silphium. Crow speculated the sorceress was about to out-sly the sly wizard. "Not a trace, Your Royal Seductress."

# CHAPTER 21

 to Florida yet, Kate asked Merlin if she could retrieve her mother's wedding ring from her aunt's apartment, and he reluctantly agreed.

Geoffrey stopped the SUV in front of the building's entrance, and Kate and Arthur got out, followed by Merlin to protect them. Even this late in the evening, four aging Latino men played dominoes on a card table under a streetlamp. Food delivery guys on electric bikes zipped this way and that, and two overweight middle-aged drunks sang "Let It Go" badly. Kate added these images to her mental scrapbook and wondered if she would remember them where she was going.

She didn't want to deal with Angry Ant, so Kate and Arthur climbed the fire escape. Merlin kept an eye on them and gathered a flock of pigeons around him.

Rita was studying on the metal platform outside her bedroom window and jumped up to hug her friend. "I thought I'd never see the gangsta's lil' boo and the gangsta himself again. Why aren't you hiding in way-back-world? Turned out to be bullshit?"

"No, we leave at dawn," Kate said.

"Well, seriously, keep your head down before takeoff, girl. You're a 'person of interest' because you hang with Art. Cops poke around all the time looking for you both."

"I'm just going to get my mother's wedding band and leave."

"Burglary from Aunt Pig," Rita said. "Count me in."

Then, she waved the Columbia University ID card with Kate's name but her own photo hanging around her neck. "Cool, huh?"

Kate laughed. "I'm glad you're me. How'd you pull that off?"

"I found the ID on my windowsill, and when I registered for classes, I discovered that you, I mean I, have a full scholarship. I thought you engineered the whole switcheroo."

"Not me."

"Who then?"

Kate put her arm around Rita's shoulder. "Maybe there's magic we don't understand."

Rita looked skeptical. "Kate, you romanced me into becoming a scientist. Don't puncture that balloon."

All three climbed to Kate's open window and entered the dark room Rita lit with her phone. Arthur opened the closet, and Kate knelt at the hem of a long winter coat. Prying the stitching loose, she retrieved the wedding ring.

The bedroom door burst open, and a shadowy figure, whose face could have been an angry Halloween mask, aimed a weapon at them. In the dim light, the gun appeared huge. "Don't friggin' move!" Peg snapped on the overhead light, and when she saw her niece, she lowered the automatic. "What are you doing sneaking into my apartment? I could have killed you."

"I came to get Mom's ring."

"You hid it from me, you ungrateful witch!"

"You would have sold it, you thieving bitch."

"Hand it over now. Gimme!"

Kate didn't, so Aunt Peg raised her gun. Arthur stepped between them.

"Oh, the big hero," Aunt Peg sneered.

"Don't do it, Kate!" Arthur yelled.

When Aunt Peg shifted her view to Kate, Arthur yanked her gun from her hand. Realizing Arthur shouted her name to create a diversion, Kate spun to karate-kick the phone out of Aunt Peg's other hand. The raised-eyebrow look exchanged between Kate and Arthur showed their surprised delight about how intuitively they'd acted in unison. Then, one-two-three, they threw the weapon and the phone out the window.

"You worthless pieces of shit," Peg spat out.

"Never talk to the king of England with such disrespect!" Kate said in her best regal, contemptuous voice. "His Majesty King Arthur and I are moving into his Camelot castle with clothes made from the finest silks and crowns festooned with exquisite gems."

"And many servants will attend our most self-indulgent whims," Arthur added, earning a congratulatory fist bump from Kate. She ceremoniously slid the ring next to the wedding ring Arthur had made with Merlin's 3D printer. Then, Kate extended her arm to her aunt. "You can kiss my ring."

"You can kiss my ass. I should've shot you both when I had the chance."

Rita laughed as Kate and Arthur climbed out the window. "The kick-bony-butt dynamic duo! But 'festooned'?"

"A fancy word for 'decorated.' I learned it studying for the college admissions test."

"Well, I'm pleased to discover that polite, serious Kate has developed some rockin' attitude. I was planning to watch a blow-up-everything movie later, but abetting fugitives might look good on my resume."

Climbing down the fire escape, Kate didn't look back. No love lost for the world's worst aunt. No love lost for the world where she was a "person of interest."

*Geoffrey drove down Lexington Avenue* with Arthur in the front seat, and Kate, Rita, and Merlin squeezed into the back.

Closing his eyes, Arthur imagined Camelot's green fields and dense forests. *I'm going home!* The land where his parents and ancestors had lived and were buried. Where acting on his instincts and values would not be criminal or categorized as a mental deficiency.

Rita leaned her head on Kate's shoulder. "You've probably used your ESP thing to sense what I'm wondering?"

Kate nodded. "Why am I going backward?"

"For sure! You're a forward person, Kate. Where you're going, 'science' is superstition and misinformation."

"I've got this wonderful tingling sense of anticipation. Like what explorers must feel. That just over the horizon, there'll be something so amazing that no matter how difficult the journey, what I discover will make the world a better place and me a better person. I'd mapped out every inch of my life, but that was someone else's program. I'm flying into the unknown where I'm going to meet new and maybe dangerous challenges that I hope to face with courage and wisdom, not just book smarts."

"Like your heroine pilot Amelia?"

"Yeah, except not the crash into the ocean part."

Geoffrey stopped at the ornate Art Deco entrance to the Chrysler Building, and Merlin got out. No trace of the sorceress's distinctive scent. The sidewalks were empty this late at night except for a woman who waited at a nearby bus stop, framed in a pool of light from an overhead streetlamp.

At the sound of Merlin's door closing, the woman turned and smiled, revealing a gap in her front teeth. He gasped. *Is it her?* Had he finally found Clarissa?

Arthur, Kate, and Rita got out, but Geoffrey hesitated. Kate stuck her head in the passenger side door. "You coming?"

"I hate flying."

She laughed and gently pulled him out. "Who doesn't!"

Merlin hustled the group into the lobby and crowded them into an elevator. The night guard protested until Merlin waved his hand over the man's eyes, leaving him with a blank stare." Merlin pushed the button for the sixty-first floor, then stepped back into the lobby as the elevator doors closed. "I'll be with you soon."

"*Is it really you?*" the gap-toothed woman asked. "Merlin?"

Her violet eyes still astonished him. Her voice still had that lovely sing-song lilt forever recorded in his brain. Although he didn't think it was possible, she had grown more beautiful with age. "Clarissa!"

She threw her arms around him. "Staying in the present without you was the dumbest decision I ever made. But now you're here! And so young and handsome!"

"I've thought of little else besides you since traveling to this time, and I have to go with you now."

She pressed against him, and his body responded to her heat. But his mind remained cool. It was an unsettling coincidence that he would find her hours before dawn time travel. And how did she know that the celestial event propelling them back to Camelot was occurring soon? And where was the mysterious speck of yellow in her right eye like Clarissa? Then he knew. Morgan had shape-changed into his long-lost love, further disguising herself with an overpowering floral perfume covering the hint of silphium that always emanated from the sorceress.

"I have a room in a hotel nearby," she whispered.

His elusive enemy was close, and to prevent her from disrupting time-traveling Arthur back to Camelot, Merlin had to keep her close and develop a plan.

*In the hotel elevator,* Merlin schemed to maneuver Morgan/Clarissa into the hotel room where she was leading him and conjure a spell to keep her there.

Morgan/Clarissa tapped her key card on a door lock in the lavishly decorated hotel corridor. Merlin stepped back, indicating with his arm for her to enter. "After you, my darling."

She stepped aside. "In the modern world, gentlemen can go first."

When he hesitated, Morgan/Clarissa playfully wrapped her arms around him from behind. "We can go in together." She quickly separated, jumping up athletically to kick him into the room. He lurched forward, snared in an intricate spiderweb.

The strawberry-blonde morphed into flaming-redheaded Morgan, wearing the green robe she had on when she arrived from Camelot. The sorceress telescoped her arm to lift Merlin's sapphire pendant off his neck, and directed her spider to crawl off the web into its home in the mouth of her golden snake bracelet. "Ta-ta for ... well, not for now. For-ever," she triumphed as she sashayed out of the room. Merlin struggled to free himself, but without his gem, his strength was diminished. *My apprentice outplayed me! Phew!*

The more he struggled, the more he became entangled. Then he stretched a finger to touch the web. Focusing his magic on it, the silk threads glowed red. But Morgan's spell on the web was stronger than his power. The effort tired him, and he paused to take deep breaths. A fly buzzed around his head and got stuck in the web. *Pigeons eat flies!* Merlin pointed his finger at a window to raise it. Closing his eyes, he mentally summoned the birds. Within minutes, a flock of pigeons fluttered into the hotel room, the boldest one gobbling up the fly. *Cut the thin web strands with your beaks, my friends. Save me and the world.*

The dutiful birds got to work freeing him.

*Morgan strode along the sidewalk* outside the hotel with Merlin's sapphire dangling around her neck. Crow landed on her welcoming extended arm. *An unprecedented gracious act.* "You're going to put glamour back into time travel, Your Royal Majesty."

Morgan patted Crow's head affectionately. "Are you coming?"

"You don't command?"

"I'm getting sentimental in my old age."

"Well, there's this little ditty from ancient times about a baker who made a pie with four and twenty blackbirds. So it doesn't sound like an ideal environment for a crow."

"After I've crushed the nobles' rebellion, there'll be plenty of rotting human flesh for you."

"A gourmet treat for sure, but my act doesn't play well with the hicks in the sticks."

"I've come to appreciate your cynicism and lack of sincerity. Crow, let's you and I have some fun and kill Arthur."

*Killing her half-brother is her idea of fun? I've much to learn about royalty,* Crow thought.

# CHAPTER 22

**O**N THE SIXTY-FIRST FLOOR, not far from the Buddhist shrine that protects them from Morgan's magic, Arthur, Kate, Rita and Geoffrey stood at a window watching the eastern sky for signs of sunrise. Now, there was a faint blue promise of dawn. "This is the big moment, and the only magic your 'wizard' can make is a disappearing act," Rita said.

"It's not sunrise yet," Arthur said without much conviction.

"A con man, fraud, fake, moob, chilidog, lying mother-frigger!" Rita spat out, her words echoing off the bare walls. "Not that I care." She put her arm around Kate. "Now I won't lose my best friend."

"And I don't have to commit suicide by jumping," Geoffrey said.

"Well, if he doesn't show, then we have to move on," Arthur said.

"Move on!" Kate slapped him hard in the face. "Why did I ever believe this bullshit fantasy could happen? I love you, and this is where I wind up!" She shook her head. "There's no place for you to hide,

Arthur! There is nothing but bad options this instant, five minutes from now, tomorrow, or next year. Look at us. A bunch of fools all dressed up and no place to go!"

Kate realized the knight was missing. "Where's Lancelot?"

"He went out to the observation deck," Geoffrey said, shrugging.

Arthur didn't hesitate to leave the safety of the Buddhist shrine to go outside. Kate, Rita, and Geoffrey followed, horrified to find the knight stripped to the waist and bent over his sword that was braced on the stone decking with its point pressing against his torso.

"What are you doing!" demanded Arthur.

"When a knight est disgraced, he must fall on his sword to end his despicable life.

"Lancelot!" Kate yelled. "The king and England needs your protection. I need you to be my friend. Stop!"

Her concern made him straighten up enough that Arthur could kick the upturned sword away. The knight crumpled to the deck in a heap. "Stand, Sir Lancelot of the Lake!"

"I est not worthy to stand in front of thee."

Looking down at the once-mighty warrior, Arthur felt that he, too, had been knocked to the mat because Merlin had abandoned them. In karate matches, he'd always get up to keep battling. But this fight, this journey, this adventure to Camelot appeared hopeless. As Kate's slap had startled him, the realization that he had not made a plan B was frighteningly disturbing.

Suddenly Merlin burst onto the deck. "Why are you all just standing there?" He pointed. "East is that way! Hurry!"

There was no time to ask where he'd been and why he was so late. Arthur pulled Lancelot to his feet, and they all ran around the corner of the building toward the glowing blue and red horizon.

"Arthur, you stand on my left with Kate," Merlin said. "Lancelot on my right. Let's see some smiles of anticipation! Come, Geoffrey. No time for worries. Hold hands and relax. Deep breaths. Next stop, Camelot!"

Arthur and Kate shared a look. "Alive or dead, we'll be together forever," Kate said.

"We're not going to die," Arthur assured her.

"Okay then. But I won't apologize for slapping you until we are safely in Camelot."

Geoffrey waved goodbye to Rita and gripped Kate's other hand. She noticed both their hands were shaking. Arthur looked up as the first rays of sun hit the spire high above them. "It's happening!"

Quivering with anticipation, Arthur didn't notice the spider creeping out of the golden snake bracelet concealed under Merlin's robe, nor did he feel it crawling on his skin. He did feel the piercing pain when the spider sank its fangs into Arthur's forearm. He winced and was stunned to see his arm instantly swelling. "What the …"

Kate swatted the spider away and stomped on it. Rita yanked off her belt and wrapped it around Arthur's arm as a tourniquet to slow the poison from attacking his vital organs. Arthur began to gasp for air. "Sit and try to remain calm, Art," Rita said.

"Arthur," Kate corrected.

Merlin shape-changed into Morgan Le Fay. "The only kingdom you'll rule is the underworld!" she shouted at her half-brother. Before Lancelot could pull his sword, Morgan pointed a finger. That froze his weapon in its sheath so firmly that, even with his enormous strength, he couldn't remove it. She leaped up, tight-roping along the top of the parapet to sit astride the stainless-steel eagle's head.

Rita dialed 911 on her cell. "We need a bus on the sixty-first-floor observation deck at the Chrysler." She succinctly described the spider bite and how the patient was breathing with difficulty.

"Sounds like you're on the job," the female 911 dispatcher said.

"EMT trainee without equipment."

"NYFD caught the call. Delta response. Be there in minutes. Hang in there, kid."

Kate and Lancelot helped Arthur sit and prop his back against a wall, and he closed his eyes. Rita gently slapped his face. "Stay with us, Art!" His eyes opened, but just as slits.

Morgan drank a potion from a small vial and reached for the sapphire hanging around her neck but paused to look south, the "city that never sleeps" spread out before her. Trucks, cars, and buses filled the streets even at this pre-dawn hour. It was as if the city's bustling energy was calling her. *Magnificent!* She rubbed the glowing sapphire as the first rays of the sun struck her and the eagle's head. Simultaneously, a comet ripped open the sky, and the sculptured bird exploded free from the masonry. Morgan rode it skyward with hypersonic speed, her flaming hair flowing behind as if she, too, were a comet. Then, in a burst of light, the sorceress disappeared into the past.

Rita checked Arthur's pulse while Kate held his sweat-covered hand. *How can I live without his energizing affection, companionship, and love? If he dies, so do I.*

It seemed like hours before the EMTs arrived. But it was probably only minutes when a tall man with a mustache that curled up on both sides of his mouth and a gray-haired woman covered with tattoos rolled their equipment-covered gurney out of the elevator.

Rita pointed out the spider bite while the man put a blood pressure cuff on Arthur's other arm. The woman said, "An anaphylactic reaction," yanking an EpiPen from her medical kit with her tattoo-covered arms. She injected the antidote into Arthur's bicep. Then she placed an oxygen mask over Arthur's nose and mouth to help him breathe.

"Been on the job twenty-two years, and I've never seen a spider bite that potent," Mustache said.

The drug quickly counteracted venom and the constriction in Arthur's throat loosened. The pure oxygen rejuvenated him. Opening his eyes, he said through the mask, "That was interesting."

The tattooed EMT turned to Rita and arched an eyebrow. "If almost dying is his idea of interesting, what does he do for excitement?"

Rita pointed to Kate with her thumb, "Ask the girlfriend."

Kate grinned. "He fights sorceresses."

"Is that a union job?" the EMT asked without cracking a smile. The tall medic with the mustache checked Arthur's blood pressure. "123 over 79."

"You're good to fight more sorceresses," the tattooed EMT said, removing the oxygen mask from Arthur's nose and mouth. "And there are probably more of them in the East Village than Midtown."

Then, she high-fived Rita. "You saved his life with that tourniquet." She and her partner packed their gear and headed for the elevators.

Refusing outstretched hands offering help, Arthur struggled to his feet just as the real Merlin shuffled onto the observation deck, his head hanging in shame.

"You betrayed us!" Arthur shouted. Despite feeling physically drained, he was clearheaded and angry. "You slammed the door shut on time travel to the one place where I could be strong and brave. In this city, in this time, I'm nothing but trash to be tossed out." He had been pushed back over the line where he no longer had the will to fight and staggered backward until Kate steadied him.

"My apology won't make things right, but I'm truly sorry. Morgan tricked me by shape-changing into Clarissa."

Kate thrust her chin at the wizard. "Look at the lives you ruined because you wanted to get laid! Lancelot's suicidal! Geoffrey dreads living the same day over and over driving his junky SUV, and Arthur'll be a convicted killer fighting for his life in jail! You broke our future, Merlin. Fix it."

To *fix it, Merlin said he needed* a pure sapphire, like the ones in the Museum of Natural History's Halls of Gems and Minerals. Arthur accompanied him on his mission to ensure Merlin's hormones didn't derail this plan.

Rita's parents were out of town at a wedding, so she took Kate, Lancelot, and Geoffrey to her apartment until the wizard found what he needed. Or not.


*The Halls of Gems and Minerals* were theatrically dark, making the well-lit stones and precious gems behind thick protective glass sparkle. Surrounded on all sides by brilliant objects, Arthur felt he was inside a jewelry box. The biggest sapphire was the Star of India inside its solitary display case in the middle of the room. The round fist-sized stone with a white star at its crown took Merlin's breath away. He could feel some of its revitalizing energy through the thick security glass. But what strength he gained was not sufficient for his magic to open the security lock. Other smaller sapphires were also protected by thick glass along the walls of the Halls. Merlin could not open any of these cases. His negative head shake was a gut punch to Arthur.

Then the wizard said brightly, "There are gem merchants not far from the hotel I stayed in. They'll have what I need."

*He's about to be stranded 1,200 years from home. Why is he so endlessly optimistic?*

On the way out of the museum, Merlin became intrigued by an exhibit entitled "Manhattanhenge." But Arthur put a restraining hand on his shoulder. "We've got to get to the jewelers now, not take a tourist stroll through exhibits."

Merlin indicated the scale model of Stonehenge with a spotlight representing the sun's rays hitting the stones at sunrise on the summer solstice. Photos of this event hung on the walls alongside dramatic videos.

"Aren't you curious about the pagan temple in the southeast area of your kingdom?" Merlin asked.

Arthur was only half listening. He and Kate had no place to live.

Sometime, somewhere, the police would collar him for sure. And all the while, Morgan would be trying to kill him.

Merlin pointed to the pictures of Stonehenge. "The Druids in ancient times were terrified of the night, believing the sun might never rise again," he told an indifferent Arthur. "They built Stonehenge to celebrate the dawn."

Merlin studied the photos of urban sunsets that lined the walls. Many showed the view facing west on Forty-Second Street and several other east–west streets. The captions explained that the setting sun aligned directly with the east–west crosstown streets several days a year in mid-spring and mid-summer. Like today. It's Manhattanhenge."

Arthur was impatient. "What the hell do I care!"

"I think we can ride the sunbeams of Manhattanhenge all the way to Stonehenge and arrive with the first rays of daylight in seventh-century England!"

"You think? You're not sure?"

"When you travel, there are no wrong turns. Only new adventures."

"Well, that new adventure won't even get to the right turn or the wrong one unless you can find a perfect sapphire," Arthur said.


*In Rita's cramped kitchen*, Geoffrey poured an inky black liquid into two coffee cups and went into the small, neat living room decorated with Broadway musical posters. The sullen knight sat on a sectional sofa while Kate and Rita cuddled in a lounge chair.

"Anyone want an espresso martini?" Geoffrey asked. "Might be the last chance to get some coffee. Where we're going, there won't be coffee or tea for another 600 years."

Rita asked, "Anyone?" No one spoke up. "I'll take that off your hands."

Rita took a sip and nodded her approval, then turned to Kate. "Well, Cinderella, I guess it's back to grade grubbing for you."

"And I never even made it to the ball."

Geoffrey sat next to the knight. "Look at the bright side, big guy. You're handsome and pious. Become a TV evangelist, and women will flock to you like moths to a flame." Lancelot didn't react. "How about the Middle East? Everyone's always fighting everyone there. I'm sure someone with as much inner anger as you could find a cause to fight for."

The knight spun around, his eyes blazing. "I shalt cut off thy ungodly tongue if thou doth not decease that twaddle!"

"Whoa, Sir Knight. Show a little grace under pressure here. I'm trying to pluck some humor from the ruins of shattered dreams."

Geoffrey stood to inspect the posters. As he stopped at each one, he mumbled the lyrics from each. Rita hummed the tunes.

"You know all the melodies," Geoffrey said. "I like the way you hummed them."

"Thanks." She smiled. "You know all the words."

"Yeah, I write musicals, so I've studied all the great shows."

"Cool. Have I seen one of your plays?"

"Not one ever produced on Broadway. Not off-Broadway, not off-off-off-Broadway."

"That sucks."

He shrugged. "You must go to the theater all the time."

"My dad's the head gaffer at many Broadway houses," Rita said. "The lighting electrician. Mom and I get free tickets to all the shows."

"He need an assistant? Just in case this time-travel thing's a flop … which I almost hope happens. I hate flying."

"Me too. But to even be an assistant, you gotta become a member of Local 52. Dad can be cranky, but he's in charge of the union apprentice program, so who knows."

Geoffrey raised a fist. "Workers of the world unite!"

Just then, Rita's phone rang, and she grabbed it. "Yeah!" She smiled. "Yeah!!" A bigger smile. "Yeah!!! I'll tell them."

"Game on, girl. Merlin bought a sapphire, but its magnetic field isn't powerful enough. He wants you to take him to the university lab with the high-powered magnets, and he also said something about riding the sunset to Stonehenge."

*Getting all six of them by the university guard* hadn't been a problem. Merlin had enough magic left to do that. But the numeric keypad lock on the fusion lab door resisted his ability to conjure the combination to unlock it.

Finally, Merlin gathered Arthur, Kate, Rita, Geoffrey, and Lancelot around him in a tight circle. "I know some of you have doubts about magic, but please, will all of you focus on the lock?"

He put his hand on the device, and no one spoke as they concentrated. Merlin could feel their energy. Numbers appeared in his head, and he pressed them into the keypad, miraculously unlocking the door.

The cavernous high-ceilinged lab was deserted on this summer Sunday. Merlin's eyes widened with curiosity at the sight of the two-story-tall circular superconductor magnet. He climbed a metal ladder to the top, pointing to the small round opening at the center. "Is this where the magnetic field will be?"

"I think so," Kate said.

He searched several pockets before finding his new sapphire and placed it in a container where the magnetism the machine generated would be transferred to the gem so Merlin could access its powers.

"We have to figure out how to turn on this monster," Kate said. She spotted a boxy structure with a glass window off to the side. She and Arthur led Rita, Geoffrey, and Lancelot inside, where they discovered the control board. Scientist Kate and Arthur studied the dials, switches, and a lever. Kate put her finger on it. "Probably to increase or decrease the power."

Arthur raised a transparent plastic cover that protected a red key. "In the movies, this is how they start complicated machines."

"Or blow everything up," Rita said.

On a microphone, Arthur pressed the "speak" button. "I think we've found the on–off key, Merlin. You'd better move away."

The wizard climbed down and joined them in the boxy structure. Arthur turned the key, the dials illuminated, and the computer screens lining the walls lit up with charts showing technical details. Rita grabbed Kate's hand. "Is this the kind of stuff you used to do in your internship lab?"

"Today is special," Kate answered.

"You got that right."

Merlin pushed the power lever forward, and the room shuddered as electricity surged into the device, slowly building its magnetic force to the max. Suddenly, the blue gem in the force field exploded. Merlin quickly lowered the power to zero. "A real sapphire would never disintegrate like that. The gem dealer sold me a fake!"

"Effing fake!" Arthur yelled.

"I willst slay the man who stole your money and went unpunished," Lancelot said.

"I'll kill him! I'm already a murderer so it makes no difference."

Kate shook her head. "Stop that shit, both of you."

A bearded professor came into the room. "What are you doing! Stay right where you are and touch nothing. I'm getting the police!" And he hurried out.

"We better vamoose," Rita said.

"No," Kate said firmly. She popped the clasp on her locket and gave her sapphire to Merlin.

"Are you sure, Kate?" Arthur asked.

"I've never been surer. It's to use when all else fails to take me home."

Merlin scurried up the metal stairs with the locket and dangled the gem over the magnet. Using the intercom, Kate told him to get away from the device, but he shook his head and yelled, "Go!"

Kate turned the key this time, and Arthur pushed the power lever to the maximum. On the lip of the superconductor, Merlin leaned forward to lower the gem inside the magnetic field. Its power made his hair and robe flutter. The gem gradually began to glow until it was lighthouse-bright. He waved to the control room, and they turned off the machine.

Kate, Arthur, Rita, Geoffrey, and Lancelot gathered around the magician, who rubbed the gem and nodded confidently. "We can ride the sunset beams to ancient England."

Two campus police, five New York City police officers, and several professors burst in. The trespassers looked around for a door or window to escape. Nothing. Merlin calmly said, "It will be okay." He then metamorphosed them into cockroaches.

"Cucaracha! Disgusting and easy on the bug spray!" Rita said.

Arthur immediately understood why Merlin had turned them into bugs. He and Merlin led Kate, Rita, Lancelot and Geoffrey into the bathroom and they all scampered to the toilet rim.

"Follow me," Arthur ordered and dove in.

"I'm not traveling down shit highway," Geoffrey squawked, so Lancelot used four of his cockroach legs to kick him into the toilet, then jumped himself.

Merlin followed. Kate saw Rita-Cucaracha hesitate. "Jump, girl!" Kate urged as she plunged in, trying to hold her cockroach nose with a tentacle. Rita dove headfirst, just before a policeman's boot thudded against the toilet.

*Crowds of New Yorkers and tourists* faced west on Forty-Second Street in anticipation of Manhattanhenge. Many held their phone cameras above their heads, ready to capture the setting sun that was now directly aligned with the east–west crosstown street. Men and women shrouded in hooded robes chanted in an ominous-sounding language. But most everyone else was in a festive mood, many with medieval-type clothes or hats made of food strainers and aluminum foil.

So, when a round utility hole cover popped open and out climbed Merlin in his robe decorated with moons and stars, Lancelot, Arthur and Kate, all in chain-mail armor, Geoffrey with a feathered hat, and Rita, no one even did a double take.

Impatient Arthur bounced on the balls of his feet, eagerly anticipating his future in the past. Lancelot knelt, but stood back up, unable to pray.

"As fate would have it, we both love the same woman," Arthur said. "I'm confident on English soil you'll regain your honor and be loyal to your Code of Chivalry and your king ... and you'll adore Kate from afar."

"Thou hath my solemn pledge."

Rita nudged her shoulder against Kate. "If you're still here after sundown, you and the king can stay at my place. Harboring a fugitive is so gangsta romantic."

"You're the best. I'm going to miss you every day, doctor."

"You'll be too busy ordering around nobles, princesses, and bishops with funny hats to want to hang with peasant girl Rita."

Kate wrapped her arms around her best friend. "Hugging in armor doesn't quite have the same tenderness," Rita said, trying not to cry.

Merlin touched Kate's glowing gem at his neck, certain of its power. The sun was disappearing into the horizon. "You better step back, Rita," the wizard said.

Rita edged away, a tear rolling down her cheek. She saw Geoffrey get coffees from a nearby taco food truck and bring them over. "Another espresso martini, gorgeous Rita?"

"Martinis from a taco truck?"

"Okay, so maybe not totally legal."

"But you need a side hustle in this town."

She took a sip, then glanced at the setting sun and grinned. "If you think getting me a drink will make me want to jump in the sack with you, we don't have enough time before you disappear. Like most guys do."

"What if I stayed?"

"You serious? You'd do that?"

"For you, yes."

"Then we'll have plenty of time," Rita said.

"The earth spins, the sun shines, and I cannot live one more moment without you, Rita."

She kissed him. "Call me Kate." She showed him the university ID with her picture on it, not Kate's. "I'm going to take her place in the world, only minus the long legs and blonde hair."

"But you've got something she doesn't. You've got attitude."

Rita/Kate ran a sensual finger down his cheek and gave him a smile that promised that in the end, he'd be pleading, "No *más*."

Merlin hung Kate's locket with the gem inside around her neck.

"Don't you need it?" she asked.

"It has shared its power with me."

*He's saying goodbye.* "No! Don't desert us, Merlin. We need you."

He kissed her cheek. "You have wisdom beyond your years, Queen Kate, and don't be afraid to act on what you sense."

Then he placed a ring on Arthur's index finger. "This is the royal seal with a Pendragon griffin that your father ordered me to deliver to you."

"But what will I do if Morgan attacks?"

"Trust you now have the strength of an eagle and the heart of a lion, Your Majesty."

A policeman had been staring at Arthur. He suddenly pulled out his semiautomatic pistol. "You in the armor. Put your hands up!" Then he yelled to a nearby officer. "This perp's a fugitive murder suspect!" The other cop pulled his weapon.

Merlin moved away from Arthur, Kate, and Lancelot's sight. The setting sun's rays shone directly along the street. Kate heard a buzzing and saw a yellow jacket wasp zipping around Arthur. What was she sensing? Before she could figure it out, a blinding luminosity enveloped her, Arthur, and Lancelot, lifting them up and carrying them to the western horizon. The speeding light disappeared through the pink and red sunset into the past.

Geoffrey and Rita clinked their coffee cups and sang a sad farewell duet.

The officers stared in disbelief. "Did we see what we just saw?" one asked. "Ummm," his partner mused. "'Suspect disappears in a lightning bolt?' Sarge wouldn't believe us if we reported it." They both holstered their weapons. "Only in New York."

England
773 CE

# CHAPTER 23

THE HULKING STONE SLABS arranged in a circle at the pagan temple called Stonehenge were ghostly pale in the pre-dawn blue hour. Then, the rays of sun marking the summer solstice shone through the pillars. A ball of pure white light seemed to ride the beams into the temple's center where Arthur, Kate, and Lancelot emerged from the brightness.

They were disoriented, looking this way and that to see where and when they had landed. "Do you think we're really in ancient England?" Kate asked.

Lancelot didn't have any doubt. He lay on the ground, pressing his body into the soil and murmuring a prayer of thanks. Arthur nodded toward the knight. "Lancelot certainly does, and he's our eyes and ears here. So, yes, we're in ago."

They held each other's hands, and he asked, "You okay?"

"Nothing hurts. I have my senses. I think. Maybe a little dizzy, but my mind is clear. How about you?"

"Great!" Arthur felt full of purpose and was eager to get started. Along with Merlin and Lancelot at the horse farm, he and Kate had mapped out a plan. First, visit his parents' burial site, then travel to Lancelot's family's Castle Ban, where Excalibur was buried deeply in an iron anvil. There, Arthur would free the sword to prove he was the legitimate king. Then, using the castle as his base, he would forge the nobles who opposed Morgan into a unified army to destroy her.

"Lead us into your world, Lancelot," Arthur said.

The knight realized the wizard wasn't in the pagan temple, nor was Geoffrey. "We hath to wait 'til the wizard arriveth."

"He stayed in the present," Arthur said.

Geoffrey's absence was no loss. But Merlin! It worried the knight not to have those magical powers to help protect the king. But as usual, he hid his emotions.

That his tutor Merlin believed the young king ready to make his own decisions boosted Arthur's confidence. But he was also just a bit nervous. Kate sensed this combination of feelings and imagined it was what adventurers experienced when setting out into the unknown. "Remember Amelia Earhart's letter I read to you describing her first solo flight. She was anxious she'd fail but also felt energized to be at the controls of her plane, and her life. I'll fly beside you, but you're the pilot."

Arthur took in a deep breath of the pure air unpolluted by centuries of civilization. Scanning the low rolling hills, everything looked crisp and bright. He wondered if his sight and hearing were more acute just as his smell was keener. Did his responsibility as king require that his senses and intellect always be on high-alert? He heard a bee buzzing around the wildflowers and pointed out the black-and-yellow insect to Kate. "The same insects as in New York."

The bee made her feel something. At first, she wondered if it was the calmness and security she was experiencing. But she wasn't sure. Time travel had disrupted the certainty about what she sensed. Hopefully, becoming more accustomed to the new images and sensations would clarify her intuition.

A sweet, sulfurous odor made Arthur's body stiffen. "When Morgan attacked me on the patio, I detected this scent. She must be near."

Lancelot picked some yellow wildflowers and held them to his nose. "'Tis silphium, a common plant that hath the same aroma as the sorceress."

Kate perceived an unseen threat. Looking around, she spotted the source of her concern. A blue jay with unusual black head feathers instead of blue perched atop one of the vertical stone slabs. It flew away after they started walking toward Castle Ban. Kate pointed. "Is that just a regular bird, or is it trouble?"

Arthur saw no menacing swooping eagles, no approaching soldiers or knights, and no sorceress. The low, rolling hills covered with tall grasses gently swaying in a cool breeze could not have been more pleasing. Bursting with energy and not burdened with doubt, he smiled at Kate. "Let's go!"

She smiled back, and they started to run, clunking along in their armor. Lancelot joined them, and all three ran with uncomplicated childlike joy.

*The jay circled a battlefield* where Morgan Le Fay's army had attacked Castle Ban, set on a hilltop at one side of a valley. A wide moat and high stone walls surrounded interior buildings, including a tall square tower. Catapults launched flaming barrels of tar that exploded on the walls and ignited internal thatched roofs. Attackers on the ground showered arrows on defenders on a stone platform protected by the castle parapet wall. But, even when the archers were protected by shields or stone walls, some soldiers were wounded or killed.

The bird flew to a large black tent strategically positioned for a view of the attacking forces and the castle. Flags decorated with a snake coiled around a scepter marked the entrance, and the jay fluttered inside where Morgan Le Fay added ingredients to a pot over an open flame. The sorceress understood the bird's raucous calls, and her glare turned icy. "Impossible!" She closed her eyes for a thoughtful moment. *Modern medicine sorcery must have saved Arthur from my spider's bite!*

"Was Merlin with them at Stonehenge?"

Its beak shook back and forth.

Morgan motioned to a bodyguard to strap on her black steel breastplate. Like the other pieces of her protective armor, it was decorated with intricate inlaid gold designs. Extravagance was her hallmark. The ebony tables and chairs were gold-trimmed, and gold candlesticks could have decorated a modern-day presidential suite. But few New York City hotels had leopard and lion hide bed quilts.

"Reginald!" Morgan yelled.

A middle-aged man with a patch over one eye slithered in so quickly he must have been hovering near the entrance. He bowed low. "Yes, Your Majesty?"

"Arthur has returned."

"From the dead?"

"Get my horse, idiot."

"I shall gather your personal guards also, Your Royal Majesty."

A longbow with a quiver hung from a tent pole, and Morgan pulled out an arrow, scraping its tip across her thumbnail to test its razor sharpness. "Merlin's not there to protect Arthur." She plunged the metal into the bubbling liquid and stirred it gently. "It'll be sooo emotionally nourishing when my lips drink from the chalice of revenge."

*Arthur, Kate, and Lancelot* had slowed to a walk in this farm country, and the king was pleased to see the knight brimming with energetic determination. City-kid Kate knew little about farming, but was it odd that a wooden plow looked abandoned in a half-cultivated field? The smell of the recently tilled soil reminded her of her horse camp, where Connecticut farmers used tractors to plow their fields not far from the fenced riding rings. She wondered how long the sights, sounds, and smells in the seventh century would transport her back to the world she left behind.

Lancelot's mood darkened when he detected the bitter odor of smoldering fire. He strode to the top of a low hill, discovering a rural village below that was totally destroyed. Normally self-controlled, Lancelot howled an enraged battle cry.

They followed the road into the ruins where fire glowed inside thatched roofs, and a cloth doll hung limply from a noose dangling from a tree limb. Not a house or building remained standing. Flames licked the skeletons of structural beams that were the only indication a structure had once stood there. Arthur's jaw muscles hardened. Merlin and Lancelot had brought him back to ancient England to stop this malicious destruction.

Inside one of these smoky shells, a gray-haired woman, appearing ghostly covered in white ashes, sat on an upside-down wooden tub. Mumbling to herself.

Kate went over. "What's wrong?" She immediately realized how dumb that question was. Everything was wrong. Nothing was right.

"Go back!" the old woman croaked. She raised a bony finger to point in the direction they were walking. "Where Morgan La Fay ruleth, the living envy the dead." Then, she laughed hysterically.

"The crone est *develseoc*, sire," Lancelot said, using the ancient term for insane. Arthur also dismissed the warning as mutterings of a deranged mind. But it reminded Kate that the modern concepts of restraint and pity did not exist where they were going. Death might be closer in their futures than she hoped.

At the edge of the village, a tall, skinny teenager with a mop of filthy hair shoveled dirt on a grave. He stabbed a sword into the soft earth and leaned a knight's shield against it.

Then, he jogged over to Lancelot and Arthur, offering to become a squire. The knight pompously told the peasant that only the sons of noblemen were worthy of becoming his squire. And that King Arthur would have many educated disciples to serve him in Camelot. The young man bowed to Arthur. "Everyone hath awaited thy return."

Arthur and Lancelot continued on their journey, but Kate looked back. How did this boy with a dirt-smeared face and tattered clothes know that Arthur was the king? No one told him. Arthur didn't wear a crown. *Was the country child one of the people with ESP in this time that Merlin told me about?*

The blazing afternoon parched their throats, and they had not passed any streams or ponds. Arthur heard a rattling and creak of wood on wood and saw a dilapidated cart pulled by a sorrowful donkey approach over a low rise. The shaggy-haired teenager was driving, and he stopped. After bowing to Arthur, he offered a drink from a water carrier made of sewn animal hide. "'Tis not a royal coach, but better than sweaty walking in this heat."

"What is your name, driver?"

"Edmund, sire."

Arthur climbed in. "It's a royal coach as soon as I sit in it."

Kate and Lancelot also got in. As they rumbled over a rutted dirt road, the youth told them about how cruelly Queen Morgan ruled. Lancelot became visibly agitated upon hearing details of the horrors and deprivations her soldiers committed, and the knight jumped off the cart to stride angrily along.

*Riding at full gallop*, Morgan and Reginald followed the black-crested blue jay along a country path. Up ahead, she saw the donkey cart and laughed. "The dishwasher's ass is riding in a dung cart pulled by an ass. Crow would appreciate the irony."

Unslinging a bow from her shoulder, she pulled the poison arrow from her quiver. "Find the mark without fail, darling darling." From this distance to the target, a regular archer must aim in a high arc, but Morgan's arrow's path was unnaturally level. Gravity had no command on its shaft because it flew on the wings of sorcery.

Kate sensed it first. Her sharp eyes spotted the weapon streaking toward them. "Arrow!" she yelled, brandishing her dagger. Without protective armor, the young squire jumped up to stand in front of the king so the arrow would hit him instead, but Arthur pushed him aside. Lancelot and Kate both missed deflecting the projectile with their daggers. Arthur deftly flicked his, cutting the arrow in two so the pieces fell harmlessly to the ground.

Morgan and Reginald were still far away but galloped toward them. *What to do?* The sorceress's arrow hadn't killed him, so Morgan would use other lethal magic. Merlin wasn't here to protect or advise, but his lessons had been well learned. Chess! Anticipate the opponent's options. Predict future outcomes. What he must do became evident in a flash.

He fell from the seat as if he had been wounded. Lying on the ground, he grabbed the arrow pieces, avoiding the tip that was clearly poisoned based on the instantly destroyed grass where it landed. He muscled the jagged broken edges around his armor into his neck so that the point protruded from one side and the stabilizing feathers from the other. It appeared as if the arrow had gone right through his neck. Blood seeped out of the wounds onto his armor.

"What are you doing!" Kate demanded.

"Mourn as if I am slain. I don't think Morgan will murder you."

*Don't think?* Kate wasn't so sure as she watched the approaching sorceress.

"I will fight her to the death," Lancelot vowed.

"Our country needs you to live to fight another day, Sir Knight. Do as I command!"

Kate knelt by him, wailing, sobbing, and Lancelot prayed. Edmund bent close to the king, gently covering his nose and mouth with his hand. It appeared to Kate that Arthur had stopped breathing. *What happened?* This terrified her more than her fear of the sorceress who reined her horse to a stop close to the body. Kate yelled, "You killed the man I love! Murderer!"

The sorceress quickly dismounted and strode toward Arthur. Kate tried to block her way, horrified Morgan would discover Arthur was playing dead. The sorceress pushed her aside and lifted Arthur's head by his hair. Satisfied he was dead, she let it drop. "No modern medicine to save your ass in my time, bro."

Lancelot thought the best way to protect the king was to destroy his enemy. Morgan was close enough. *Plunge my sword through her breastplate armor and silence her godless heart.* He thrust with a lightning stroke. Without even looking at the knight, she pointed a finger, and the strong Damascus steel blade drooped, as lethal as a wet bath towel. "See what happens when you go against a real woman, big boy."

Telescoping her arm until it wrapped around his neck, she pulled Lancelot close, almost in an embrace. Grabbing powder from a leather pouch, she threw it into his face. Staggering backward, fiery pain made Lancelot clamp his eyes shut. When he was able to force them open, all he saw was darkness.

"I'd invite you to witness how I'm destroying your father's castle, but … whoops, the no-seeing thing will make that a problem." Morgan mounted her horse and said to Kate, "You feel your mind powers growing, sister," the sorceress said matter-of-factly. "There will be a time when you willingly sit at the foot of my throne so you can learn from me how to fulfill your heart's aching for respect."

Kate sobbed and pressed her cheek to Arthur's blood-smeared breastplate. "Never."

"Never believe in never. Things change." Morgan turned her horse around and galloped off, with Reginald desperately racing to catch up.

Kate's throat tightened in panic when she still didn't hear Arthur breathing. Edmund cradled the king's head and again touched Arthur's face. Finally, Arthur exhaled as if he had been holding his breath all this time. Kate, too, took a breath of relief, and wondered if the shaggy-haired kid might have magic.

Arthur sat up and pulled the arrows from his neck.

"Quick thinking, Mr. King!" Kate said as she wrapped a scarf over the wounds. While he was pleased his plan had tricked the sorceress, he was troubled that his guide in ancient England was staggering around defenselessly. The king gently held the knight's arm. "Can you see anything?"

"Only blackness."

It was the only time Arthur had heard fear in Lancelot's voice.

Hoping that rinsing Morgan's poison might restore his sight, Kate found water in a nearby stream and gently flushed Lancelot's eyes. Her face was only inches from his. It was unsettling how her body heated as she touched the warrior's surprisingly soft skin. Even with the last traces of the powder flushed away, his eyesight didn't return.

Without Lancelot's vision, Arthur and Kate were lost in a world without maps or road signs. Who could they trust? Would they accidentally stumble into Morgan's soldiers and be captured?

"I knoweth the way, Your Majesty," Edmund offered. "I can guide you to Castle Ban."

*How did he know what I was thinking?* Arthur wondered.

*Edmund drove the donkey cart* along a narrow path in a dense forest. Arthur sat next to him with Lancelot and Kate in the back. She reached out to hold the knight's hand, imagining he would want human connection in his sightless world. But he pulled away.

A snake slithered toward the cart, then disappeared into the thick woods. "A black snake!" Arthur said. "Is it poisonous, Lancelot?"

Sitting rigidly, the knight was consumed by despair. *If Morgan's siege of our castle is successful, she'll murder my father, mother, and all the nobles who oppose her. Without sight, I est useless. Blindness surpasseth death.*

When the knight didn't answer, Edmund told Arthur, "Black snakes art welcome everywhere, inside castles too. They doth consume rats."

Arthur released the pressure on his dagger. *Easy does it.* "I keep wondering how much more experience it will take until I know what puts us in danger or is just a harmless snake," he said to Kate.

"I have the same worry. And for us to learn the difference will be a lot more difficult without ..." She pointed to Lancelot's eyes.

They drove by a swamp that Lancelot detected by the rotten scent of plants aptly called skunk cabbage. "Merlin's dwelling est nigh. If—"

Kate finished his sentence. "If he were here, he could make an antidote."

"You're a chemist, Kate. Go for it!" Arthur said.

"Maybe he made notes about his potions."

Even this remote possibility of a cure eased some of Lancelot's despair. "At the giant oak tree, proceed left, though there appeareth no path or trail."

The forest grew increasingly denser. Branches and vines hung low to the ground, and a strong wind swirled around them, seemingly assaulting the travelers. A high-pitched shriek startled Kate. *Was that the sorceress who had morphed into an eagle?* Above, a blue jay emerged from its hiding place, frantically darting this way and that. A falcon swooped down and attacked with such violence that the jay disappeared in a feathery explosion, then fell dead to the ground.

"Doth a peregrine falcon or kestrel slay a crow?" Lancelot asked.

"I think it was a blue jay," Arthur said.

"Like the one at Stonehenge," Kate said.

"Merlin's personal falcons and owls keepeth his workshop secret from the sorceress's spying birds. We est safe here."

The falcon slowly descended to fly near Kate.

The knight tilted his head to locate and identify a sound. "I heareth wings aflutter. Doth raptors favor Kate as they favor Merlin?"

"So it appears," she said and held out her arm like she had seen falconers do in videos. The raptor landed gently so its yellow talons didn't puncture her skin. *Did it just nod hello to me?* Even with her sizable vocabulary, she had no words to describe her profound feeling of closeness with this wild bird. "Yes, we have lots to learn," she said to Arthur.

Edmund continued driving into an area where bright orchids and plants with radiantly colored leaves mixed with dense green foliage and rotting fallen dead trees. Although there was no house or structure, Kate said, "Merlin's home is here."

The cart stopped near a green mound that rose abruptly from the ground. Lancelot slid off the end of the cart and started walking toward it but stopped, unsure of his direction.

"Does moss cover Merlin's house?" Kate asked.

He nodded, and she guided him to the structure, where he searched under the moss with his hand and brushed the plants aside to expose a metal latch. Then, with a touch of his finger, a door swung open.

*Where Merlin lived could hardly be called* a home. Venison pies laid half-eaten here and there. The bookshelves were filled, and thick leather-bound books were stacked haphazardly on the bed and chairs. Vials and beakers filled with colorful liquids and bowls overflowing with cut-up herbs and plants were stored in no apparent order in cabinets. An apparatus for heating ingredients sat on a table crowded with more vials and an open book where the wizard had written detailed notes of his experiments in Latin. Kate felt lightheaded and had to steady herself by leaning against the wooden table. Phew. This is where Merlin's crude scientific methods collided and expanded with his magic. Did she hear his voice, or was his spirit so strong in his laboratory that it seemed he was actually here? She took a deep breath. Was the formula for an antidote to Morgan's evil blinding-dust somewhere in these books?

Lancelot slumped against a wall, useless and defeated, so he was no help. Kate studied one year of high school Latin and struggled translating.

"Can I be of service?" asked Edmund. "May I translate?"

"That would be very helpful," Kate answered.

He read one book with no formula that would help.

The sun went down, and the room darkened until candles magically lit themselves one by one. Kate and Edmund continued searching through the night. Her stomach rumbled with hunger. Which one of these volumes held the secrets? She had no idea and stared blankly, paralyzed by indecision.

Edmund picked up a thick book with a tattered cover. "Shall we try this one, Your Highness?"

She shrugged. It was as good as any of the other hundreds spread out around the room.

Toward the middle of that volume, Kate and Edmund found a potion formula Merlin had concocted for a peddler blinded by a witch who'd felt cheated. The ingredients for the potion were in Latin, and she read aloud the names of ancient English herbs, plants, and animal parts. Edmund began to translate until Lancelot emerged from his stupor to use his knowledge of Latin and local foliage.

Edmund located the herbs, roots, and animal parts stored in the chaotic workspace. She ground the ingredients with a mortar and pestle, mixed it with bat blood and water, then heated it over a small fire until it bubbled. *Like how they make potions in the cartoons,* Kate thought.

It was dawn by the time she had removed the foul-smelling mixture from the heat and cooled it. "Okay, here goes." Kate wet a cloth in the mixture and gently applied it to Lancelot's eyes. They waited. No sight. She daubed on more potion. Nothing.

Kate reread the wizard's notes and shook her head in puzzlement.

Edmund smelled several of the plants. "These seem old. Maybe fresher ones will be more potent. I will see what I can find in the forest."

*How does a peasant boy know Latin and have the ability to detect staleness in plants? But then, so much was strange here.*

*The next morning, eager to join the fight* against Morgan, impatient Arthur paced back and forth outside Merlin's work home. When Kate came out, he demanded, "Did you make a potion to regain Lancelot's sight, or did you give him a sleeping pill that drugged him way past sunrise? Get him moving."

Kate stepped close, her chin almost touching his. "I'm your bride-to-be, and I'll love you 'in sickness and in health till death us do part.' But forget commanding me."

Arthur's cheeks flushed with anger. That subsided when the knight strode out of the moss-covered door with no blind-man hesitancy. However, Lancelot did shake his eyes from the bright sunlight with a hand. Arthur held five fingers in front of his face. "What do you see, Sir Knight?"

"Morgan Le Fay with her head asunder."

Kate fist-bumped with Edmund, who shyly bowed. Then, the queen grinned at Arthur and raised her eyebrows. "Hocus-pocus."

# CHAPTER 24

KING UTHER'S and Queen Igraine's tomb was en route to Castle Ban, and as they bumped along a rutted dirt road, the usually taciturn knight enthusiastically described the royal memorial chapel. It was modeled on the beautiful cathedral at Canterbury and built by the finest masons. Bishops and nobles from all over England attended the burial, and he and five honorable knights carried the king's casket to its final resting place inside the sacred building. Arthur was increasingly impatient to see where his parents were buried.

The sun was almost at its noon peak when Lancelot directed Edmund to drive off the dirt road into a clearing. The sight of building stones, columns, and broken Christian crosses scattered about made Lancelot's eyes darken and his face twist into a mask of sadness and outrage. "'Tis Morgan that has pillaged the royal mausoleum!"

Kate knew Arthur's dream of finding his parents had haunted him all his life. He had come to pay his respects and quietly commune with their spirits. But there was no peace here. Upon seeing these violated graves, she could hardly imagine the quantum chaos of his emotions. His winter-cold facial expression revealed no inner disappointment or turmoil. Still, she sensed he was about to explode with rage. "I'm so sorry," Kate whispered.

The grass had been set aflame, and no sprouts had grown through the ashes. Remnants of stone walls, gravel paths, colorless dead flowers, and uprooted shrubs were ghostly indications of formal gardens that once surrounded the monument. No birds sang. It was too desolate for them or any other animal. Arthur strode into the ruins, where two tarnished bronze caskets seemed curiously out of place in what was now an open field. A prone bronze head-to-toe sculpture of his mother was on top of her undamaged casket. Even if his parents were alive, he expected no apologies or explanations. As a boy, he had abandoned wishing to experience parental encouragement or affection. By coming to their graves, he hoped he would feel some connection and maybe discover some emotion other than resentment at being exiled to New York. He placed his hand on the queen's statue where her heart would have been. But felt nothing.

King Uther's overturned casket was empty, mirroring the hollowness Arthur felt in his gut. His father wasn't present in death as he hadn't been in life. What Arthur experienced was not so much grief but a sense of lost opportunity. He wished he could share his few accomplishments that would make his parents proud. And would they have loved Kate even though she wasn't from a noble family? Would they have loved him? Important unanswered questions that would linger forever.

It took all Arthur's strength to tip the king's casket upright and wrestle open the heavy lid on top. The sculpture of King Uther holding his sword had been savaged beyond recognition. Arthur held his hand over the demolished likeness but didn't touch it. A feeling he had not anticipated slowly turned into a realization. If his father had not hidden him in the future, Arthur would not be standing here alive. In Camelot, baby Arthur could have had his throat slit. Merlin once told Arthur that Morgan Le Fay's mother had tried to poison him as an infant. So, *maybe his parents saved his life.* This thought lightened the bitterness that weighed so heavily on his heart.

The sun came from behind clouds, reflecting off a shiny object in the ashes surrounding the ruins. Arthur picked up an exquisitely crafted armored glove with King Uther's three griffins etched on its steel surface. *He must have been buried in his armor.* It fit perfectly, and flexing the steel-covered fingers, he gripped his sword handle. *Wonderful! How could ancient armorers create something strong yet flexible without modern forges or hydraulic presses?* Their skill seemed much more advanced than the primitive world that would be his home.

He stood erect at what he imagined had been the tomb entrance. "Hi Dad. Hi Mom. I'm going now, but I'll find Dad's body and reunite you under the roof of a new monument."

He climbed into the cart, and Kate wanted nothing more than to console him. But she couldn't find the right words, so she held his hand that wasn't covered with the steel glove. It wasn't tense, so she sensed he had made some peace with his parents' spirits.

But when he looked back at the violated burial site, she felt his fingers close into an angry fist. "Until this moment, fighting Morgan was a good and proper cause, but it was an idea," Arthur said, his jaw muscles tightening. "Now ... she has insulted my family's honor." He touched his chest. "Now, the cause is here."

*Not to mention tried to kill you at every opportunity,* Kate thought.

Hot rage boiled up in him. He exhaled and practiced slow breathing to tame his emotions. He couldn't let his anger confuse his decisiveness in battle or diminish the skill at arms he needed in order to destroy her.

*Morgan's army blocked the entrance* to Castle Ban, so Lancelot led Arthur, Kate, and Edmund to the rear of the fortress. To avoid contact with enemy forces, the knight led the group through a dense forest with no trails. Desperate to join the defense of his parents, the knight rushed ahead, knocking aside bushes and small trees with his sword. To the city-kids, every rock and tree looked the same, and Arthur, in particular, knew they would be lost in a heartbeat without their guide. So they jogged to stay close.

Arthur spotted an "L" carved into a massive tree at a child's height and figured this was the knight's childhood backyard. That's why he moved with such confidence. A little further along, Arthur stepped on a dry, dead tree limb. Picking up a piece, he was satisfied with its sturdiness and put it in a leather pouch on his belt.

Kate spotted colorful songbirds but no crows or blue jays, and when the peregrine with the yellow claws swooped down near Kate, she realized why. Her feathered protector had summoned a flock of hawks, falcons, and owls that circled high above them and in the surrounding trees to kill any of Morgan's flying spies.

Lancelot burst out of the woods into an open area at the foot of a sheer cliff, followed by Kate, Edmund, and Arthur. Not long ago, Arthur would have tried to figure out a recreational climbing route up the rock face. Now, he analyzed it as a military leader and determined it would be impossible for soldiers weighed down by armor to scale it. No wonder Morgan had staged her attack at the castle's front.

The knight inserted his dagger into a narrow crack in the stone and jiggled the blade until he heard a metallic click. He grabbed a handhold to open a door supported on massive iron hinges. Stone covered the wooden structure, and it blended into the surrounding rock so perfectly that, even up close, neither Kate nor Arthur spotted this entrance that was tall enough for a rider on horseback to enter. They all went in, and Lancelot pulled the door closed behind them.

# CHAPTER 25

BEFORE THE KING MET the nobles, the knight took Arthur and Kate through damp secret passageways filled with cobwebs to introduce them to his father, the Earl of Ban. *Am I in some sword-and-sorcery video game?* Arthur wondered, until a rat the size of a large cat bumped up against his leg. The earl's private rooms were at the top of the tallest tower with views of the castle interior and the surrounding countryside, which Morgan's army now occupied. Tapestries depicting military battles covered some of the walls, and swords, battle-axes, and other edged weapons were arranged like artwork on others. A warrior's room.

Lancelot's mother was not there to greet her son. Kate wondered if something was wrong with her health or if women were not included in seventh-century decisions.

The earl formally greeted his son, who had been on a dangerous time-traveling quest. Arthur could see they both were disciplined not to display emotion. Like his son, the earl was almost a head taller than most of the men in the seventh century. While his white hair was thinning, his shoulders were unbent by age. He politely greeted Arthur and Kate but with skepticism in his eyes that this teenager was the warrior king that could save Camelot and England.

The earl explained why Castle Ban was a prize target for Morgan Le Fay. The castle was the strongest fortress after Camelot, and the most powerful nobles who opposed the sorceress as queen were trapped inside. The earl had summoned them to plan a strategy to defeat her, and as soon as all seven had arrived with only a fraction of their personal armies, she attacked.

"One or more must be her spy," Arthur said.

The earl shook his head as if Arthur were impossibly naive. "Most certainly. But I arranged in utmost secrecy, and I knoweth these noblemen a lifetime. Brave and true knights all."

Arthur knew he would not learn anything more from this arrogant, narrow-minded aristocrat and dismissed him—earning an angry scowl from the older man.

He told Lancelot and Kate that he wished to be alone with Excalibur. Kate initially objected to being excluded from this important moment. Yet she understood he needed time alone to mentally prepare to be king.

In the castle's great room, the sword was buried deep inside a blacksmith's iron anvil in front of a fireplace large enough for a man to stand upright. Arthur admired the understated beauty of its design that exemplified the ideals of simplicity and elegance central to the

guiding principles of karate. The etching of griffins on the crosspiece between the handle and the blade was more suggestive than detailed, almost like abstract art.

He reached for the handle, then stopped. He had one inheritance from King Uther, the armored glove. He yanked the glove from a leather pouch attached to his waist and pulled it on. He opened and closed his fist. It was part of his father and now part of him. Arthur grasped the handle, and a gentle electrical current flowed into his arm. The longer he held it, the more invincible he felt. *No one can beat me!* The only time he experienced this sensation was when he defeated his opponent to win the state karate championship.

He released his grip and studied the dimly lit room. A long rectangular table stood at the other end, and a shaft of sunlight from a high window shone on it with the intensity of a spotlight. A plan to extract Excalibur and prove his royal birthright to the noblemen popped into his head. Determining where shafts of sunlight from a high window hit a large wooden table, he used every ounce of strength to heft the anvil into the bright area onto the oaken surface.

*To prepare for meeting the nobles,* Arthur had Lancelot tell him detailed individual and family histories of each man. Who had ambitions for more power? Who would gain the most if Morgan was not defeated? Arthur also directed Lancelot to gather twelve trustworthy warrior knights to become his guards.

In the great hall, the Earl of Ban, seven nobles, and Kate sat at the large table with Excalibur embedded in the anvil placed in the middle. The highest nobles had seats nearest the empty throne. As the Hand of the King, Kate had the position immediately to the king's right.

She sometimes felt another Kate was floating above her, experiencing and observing simultaneously. Certainly, the clothes and formal manners reminded her every day that she was in a vastly different era. As did the intense smells. Few of these nobles bathed, and a haze of body odor surrounded them. The stench of human waste that the servants dumped into the castle moat polluted every room. And why wasn't anyone bothered by the rats scurrying around? But what focused Kate's attention was the smoldering restlessness in these nobles unaccustomed to waiting for anyone, especially a teenager, who may or may not be king.

Heads turned when the twelve-foot-tall wooden entry doors burst open, and Arthur strode through, now wearing a white tunic decorated with three griffins. Wearing similar tunics, his twelve knights followed and positioned themselves around the nobles.

Arthur stood at the head of the table and studied these warriors who fought to remove Morgan from the throne. Their beards and hair may be flecked with white, but they were still hard men, the scars of many battles marking their faces. Their eyes were snake-cold, giving nothing, asking nothing. He'd stood before such men in assistant principals' offices and police interrogation rooms. Today, he was on the power side of the desk and liked it a lot better.

He said nothing until the silence was deafening, and the nobles were growing more restless. Then, as a shaft of sunlight dramatically reflected off the visible blade, making it appear illuminated from the inside, Arthur leaped to the tabletop, demonstrating his strength and athletic ability. He gripped Excalibur with his armored glove and braced himself. Several nobles shared skeptical glances. Mighty knights, rogues, and nobles, including many gathered here, had tried to prove they were the legitimate king by claiming the sword. All had failed.

Arthur strained, and the steel quivered. With every inch Excalibur slipped from the anvil's iron grip, more self-assurance radiated from his eyes and body. Kate detected no trace of the doubt-tormented dishwasher. He was the leader who dominated the room.

Man by man, the nobles stood and bowed. Kate curtsied, then silently clapped her hands to show appreciation for Arthur's transformative performance. He jumped down and stood at the head of the table, never sitting when he could be on his feet, ready to move. The nobles remained standing, but he motioned for them to sit. Kate smiled to herself. *Yes, control them.*

Arthur had never led a meeting nor given orders to grown men, but he'd read how generals operated, particularly Ulysses Grant. While planning battles with his staff, he rarely spoke as they suggested this strategy or that tactic. Arthur listened as the nobles explained the dire situation: the castle's food and supply of weapons were almost depleted. Morgan was preparing a battering ram that would span the moat at the castle front. When completed, the ram would shatter the drawbridge that protected the castle entrance. Her superior forces would rush in, murder every soldier, then ravish or enslave the women and children. Surrender would end with the same result.

As he absorbed this information, Arthur also visually scouted the men's body language—a self-protective instinct he'd learned living on the streets of New York. The earl had told him that he suspected one of them was a spy for Morgan but did not know which one. Do their hands form into fists? Have they stopped blinking? Do their eyes reveal a friend or foe?

Kate felt her ESP dial up and sensed that only the man wearing a tunic with *fleur-de-lis* emblems was untrustworthy. When Arthur glanced at Kate for her opinion, she indicated the spy by slyly pointing a finger. He had come to the same conclusion. "We come together to join forces against Morgan Le Fay, and we shall conquer her together. Those who sell their loyalty to the enemy will suffer. Guards!"

The king pointed Excalibur at the traitor with the *fleur-de-lis* insignia, and several guards pulled the protesting noble from his chair, dragging him toward the door. "Morgan shalt put thee all to the sword!" he yelled. "No human warrior can defy her sorcery!" He kept shouting even when he was outside the great hall. Then, he was silent.

There had been little love in Arthur's life until Kate, so he had learned not to expect or need love. He concluded that to lead in the violent seventh century, he needed to be feared. Looking at the nobles, he detected anxiety in their eyes. Like General Grant, the king ended the meeting without revealing his plans. When the time came, he would tell them how to proceed.

# CHAPTER 26

DRESSED IN HER BLACK ARMOR, Morgan studied herself in a full-length mirror where the ancient glass distorted her image. "Say, you look foxy in midnight-black armor trimmed with gold," she said to a crow perched on a wooden stand nearby. The bird just stared at her.

She cursed, angry at the stupidity of this country-bumpkin bird and at herself for missing Crow and the luxury and style of New York City. Sentimentality was for children and fainthearted grandmothers. Not the queen. But no one in Camelot possessed Crow's pretension-stripping observations or sarcastic wit. Scheming Reginald was devious enough, but his idea of humor was as funny as a finger poke in the eye. "Stupid!" she yelled at the crow.

Reginald poked his head into her command tent. "Your Majesty summoned?"

"I need a new crow. And get rid of this dolt in the usual way."

"Most certainly, Your Majesty. I shall punish the royal gamekeeper for providing you with an unteachable bird?"

"You're learning."

Reginald put the crow under one arm and hesitated before he left.

"What!" she demanded.

"There is something you might want to see."

"Besides Ban's head on a pike."

"Less dramatic. Uther's battle flag doth fly over Ban's castle, so Arthur survived and somehow est inside to display it as if he were king."

Morgan swept through the tent flap to glare at a white flag with red griffins flying from the highest castle tower. Her expression turned hawk-sharp. "You're proving hard to kill, my brother. But those stout walls trap you, and now, you're mine."

*Arthur and Kate had a candlelit bedroom* in the tower but not as high as the earl's quarters above them. Through a slit of a window in the stone walls, they could see the combat raging below. The campfires of Morgan's vast army flickered in the darkness. Arrows shot by the attackers and defenders seemed dense as flocks of angry birds, and the cries of the wounded and dying pierced the dim of battle.

Arthur sat on a wooden bench, found the branch in the leather pouch, and pulled his dagger from its sheath. Methodically, he carved off narrow strips. It was a calming activity that helped him unscramble his tangled thoughts on how to lead the peasant families, nobles, and their warriors to safety. Then, on to victory.

He was lost in thought as Kate studied his face. *Did he have doubts or negative reactions about time-traveling to what appeared to be a doomed battle and almost certain death?* But the king had become as capable as Lancelot at not displaying his emotions.

Kate didn't want to disturb his planning, so she left their room to explore the castle. In the great hall, more swords and long poles with sinister-looking spears and axe blades were displayed in a fan-like semicircle above a fireplace. Almost every man carried a sword, dagger, or both, even among allies. There is treachery and violence the castle walls cannot keep out.

Kate sensed someone watching, and when she turned to look back, a knight in armor ducked behind a wall. Lancelot? Did he think she needed his protection? Or did he want to be alone with her? She waited to see if he would approach, but he didn't show himself.

Moaning coming from inside the castle chapel distracted her. She went into the space lit by flickering torches. The stink of human waste and rotting flesh filled the air. Wounded soldiers lay on straw soaked with their blood. Country women and children seeking refuge in the castle huddled together, their eyes empty of hope. Kate wanted to help the wounded, but squalid conditions turned her stomach. Bile filled her throat, and she rushed out to vomit.

This reality was shockingly different from the glorious jousting tournaments Lancelot had described, where maidens in their finest silks admired knights displaying their fighting skills. On this dark night, there were no colorful tents or flags. Instead, there was fear and death and misery. But courage too. In the spacious exterior courtyard, archers and soldiers with shields climbed up steep steps to the parapet to join other warriors firing arrows at the enemy. To shoot, they had to expose themselves to the attackers. Such bravery! Such a waste of human life!

She returned to the bedroom to find Arthur still lost in thought. The moon rose and set. The stick had become just a splinter when he stood and looked out the window at Morgan's huge army.

He thrust his chin out. "We'll lose the battle to win the war."

"How does that work?"

"There was a brilliant French general named Napoleon, or there will be around 1800, who conquered most of Europe. Then, he attacked

Imperial Russia, driving the Russian army into retreat but failing to destroy it. The general triumphantly led his troops into Moscow, only to find the citizens had fled. Russian soldiers torched the buildings, retreated, and destroyed or carried off anything the French needed for survival. With little food or shelter for his troops, Napoleon had to march his army one thousand miles back to Europe during the brutal Russian winter. The cold killed many more soldiers than the Russian army."

Arthur sheathed his dagger. "All my knights, foot soldiers, and civilians will evacuate through the rear entrance."

"I thought it was against the knight's Code of Chivalry to retreat."

"They have no choice but to obey me."

*Of course. Art had become King Arthur.*

"Then, we'll join other nobles and warriors who have not been trapped in Castle Ban to create a force strong enough to defeat Morgan."

This fight was monumentally more important than doing extra-credit chemistry experiments in her high school lab. Here, it was kill or be killed, and Kate was more than a little surprised that she abandoned her modern-day belief that there were peaceful solutions to every conflict. She was part of a crusade against evil, the most significant challenge she had ever signed up for. And that energized her.

Arthur too. She had always believed he would unbind the chains of poverty and rejection that imprisoned him in the modern era. He was brainy and forceful in his birth country, and this century suited his personality.


*Heavy clouds dimmed the moonlight* as ghostly figures moved silently out of the secret entrance to Castle Ban. The last civilian was a young mother breastfeeding an infant so it would not cry, and Kate directed her to a partially seen trail. Next, foot soldiers in chain-mail armor marched out, holding their weapons to prevent the metal from clanging against other metal. Knights followed, their horses' hooves wrapped in cloth to muffle the sound. Arthur left only when every man, woman, and child had safely exited.

A spying blue jay perched on a castle wall was anxious to get information about this retreat to Morgan. It didn't spot any killer birds of prey, so it flew toward the sorceress's battle tent. But it didn't get far. A barn owl swooped out of low clouds, spearing the jay with deadly talons.

Arthur, Kate, Lancelot, and Edmund rode past the marching troops and civilians to the front of the evacuation, where the Earl of Ban led. This land was his estate. Even in the dark night, he knew where the path went. But he relinquished the lead to the king and Lancelot.

*Had they really slipped away without Morgan detecting their movement?* Arthur suspected the sorceress had other spies besides the birds. A breeze had blown off clouds, and the full moon's light made it easier to see. Kate thought she spotted eyes watching, then vanishing into the foliage. "Did you see something?"

Arthur had not. But then he saw a human form that disappeared without a sound. He and Kate pulled their swords. Edmund trotted up next to them. "There est no danger, sire. They wish to pay homage to their king."

"Who?"

"Forest people. This wilderness est the only place safe from Morgan's brutality."

"I will meet these forest folk."

Edmund whistled twice, which was answered by three short whistles. Hundreds of adults and children emerged from the trees and bushes that concealed them. Dressed in tattered rags, with matted hair and faces smudged with grime, they appeared to be savages, the children's stomachs distended by hunger.

Arthur understood these peasants because he had been downtrodden too. In ancient England, food was served on rounds of flat, stale bread called trenchers. So, no dishes. No dishwashers. But these wretched forest folk's lowly place in Camelot society made them the seventh century equivalent of twenty-first-century dishwashers. However tattered and powerless they looked, they had courage in their hearts and carried their simple farming tools as weapons. For the Dishwasher King, enabling these poor souls to return to their farms and shops was as compelling a mission as defeating Morgan Le Fay.

He dismounted and motioned for them to come closer. The peasants hesitated until he took the hand of a young girl missing her front baby teeth. As he walked with her, other children and adults gathered around their young, friendly king.

*The steel tip of Morgan's battering ram* slammed into Castle Ban's drawbridge. The wood splintered, and Morgan rushed through the opening. Knights on horseback and foot soldiers followed, their savage yells reverberating off the stone walls. But no army opposed her. No defiant brother. She scanned the deserted courtyard and understood why her troops had not been bombarded with flaming arrows from the parapets. The archers there were straw-filled dummies with painted human faces.

Enraged, Morgan conjured an image of Arthur and slashed it, but the apparition remained whole and unharmed, increasing her fury. Wildly hacking, she wounded one of her soldiers, who howled in pain. As his fellow soldiers carried him away, she screamed, "It's not your peasant blood I want on my sword!"

Reginald bowed. "Now, Your Majesty, we wilst fight Arthur in open fields where castle stone doth not protect him. Hence, he hath less chance of survival." He smirked. "And, after you slay him, Your Royal Majesty can killeth all opposed to thee."

She focused her fiery eyes on him, then laughed. "Reginald, you're just so upbeat about slaughter."

# CHAPTER 27

PROTECTED BY CHAIN-MAIL ARMOR, Arthur and Kate sat on their horses at the front of an army of knights, foot soldiers, and archers. The nobles from Castle Ban and others opposed to Morgan Le Fay supplied these warriors and agreed that Arthur should lead them into battle. After consulting with the lords, the young king positioned the soldiers at the highest point on a treeless field. Morgan's opposing army would have the disadvantage of fighting uphill.

Arthur surveyed the enemy formation that stretched from horizon to horizon. The rising sun tinted Morgan's knights' steel helmets bloodred, and Arthur had a startling revelation. He was seeing the reality of the dream he had experienced again and again growing up in New York. He had often wondered why he had such fierce motivation to do all the push-ups, endure the exhausting karate training, and not give in to fatigue during endless sword practices. Now, it became breathtakingly clear. At this battlefield on this day and this hour in the year 773, he had to fight Morgan Le Fay to claim the throne of Camelot, and he'd need all that disciplined strength and mental toughness from his training.

Arthur rode along the front of his battle formation to acknowledge the nobles' commitment and inspire the troops. The knights in full armor with their personal pennants attached to lances greeted him with full-throated battle cries. Then, the king dismounted to walk among the foot soldiers. They bowed with solemn, unsmiling faces. A boy carrying a bucket with a drinking gourd offered water to the men whose throats were parched with fear. Soldiers prayed or fixed identifying objects like rings or colored scarves on the backs of their chain-mail armor. *Is this some ancient superstition?* Then, it hit him. This was so their wives or mothers could identify their bodies among the dead. They weren't the knights on their magnificent steeds impatient for glory even if they had to die to achieve it. They toiled on the nobles' estates and were duty bound to fight for them and the king. These soldiers would get little or no recognition at the end of the day. There'd be only the survivors and the dead.

Across the field, groups of Morgan's knights and foot soldiers were deserting before the battle started. Reginald rode up beside Morgan, who was positioned at the head of her forces. "The Duke of Orkney and the Earl of Dartmouth wilst not oppose King Arthur, and they hath abandoned the field with their troops."

"Arthur is not king!" she yelled. "I will delight seeing those traitors drawn and quartered and their flesh fed to dogs."

*Arthur mounted his horse* between Kate and Lancelot. Dazzling in white armor, the knight was eager for battle. His belief in honor made his sense of purpose absolute, and only in combat did his extraordinary strength find release. No thinking. No either-or.

"Magnificent, sire! How the sun doth glimmer off the armor! The banners doth flutter as the ocean waves, breaking gently upon a golden shore," Lancelot said in a songlike cadence.

Kate glanced at the knight. *The promise of death and killing brings out the poet in him?*

She had never thought of herself as a fighter. Yes, she was feisty and stuck up for herself and those around her when bullied or mistreated. Yet here she was in full armor, carrying a lethal weapon. Probably the only other woman on the battlefield aside from Morgan Le Fay. But she had trained to use a sword and a shield. Although getting mortally wounded or killing another human being terrified her, she overcame those fears. Fighting at Arthur's side to overthrow the sorceress who was destroying a rural paradise was a goal more important than her own life. She might not have discovered this courage and purpose in New York. So, time-traveling to Camelot was not just to be with the man she loved. It had also become an adventure of personal discovery.

Arthur turned to look at row upon row of foot soldiers prepared to follow him into combat. How many would die or be crippled on this day? Half maybe? And what about the forest people gathered in an enthusiastic but untrained hoard behind the troops? He had ordered them to leave the battlefield, but while they most likely knew their scythes, pitchforks, and wooden staffs would be useless against lances and swords, they were determined to fight Morgan or die trying. *Even if they won, how would the glory of victory make their meager lives better? Is my empathy for my soldiers and citizens weakening me and jeopardizing my will to thrust them into combat?* Merlin wasn't there to advise. He had to decide.

Arthur closed his eyes to imagine different strategies and tactics. Even if he led his forces to victory, there would be many deaths. However, there was one choice of action that could defeat the sorceress and save lives. Single combat. He was certain this was the correct decision.

He also knew that if he didn't act immediately, doubts would creep in and dull his effectiveness. "Wait here," he told Kate and Lancelot.

"What are you doing!" she demanded.

"Cut off the head, and the snake dies. I alone will fight Morgan."

"She wilt beckon sorcery, sire," Lancelot said.

Arthur did not heed the knight's warning because, in his head, Arthur heard Merlin's voice assure him: *You have the strength of an eagle and the heart of a lion!* He unsheathed Excalibur and galloped forward. Behind him, the troops cheered and chanted his name.

Astride her horse, Morgan grinned as her half-brother rode toward her. "Ah, he offers single combat," she said to Reginald. "I couldn't wish for more!"

Arthur knew she was excited to fight by her exuberance as she galloped toward him, her hair trailing behind like a billowing red cape. The sorceress and Arthur stopped their horses between the armies. "It's just you and me, Morgan!" he said.

"Delightful, but I'm disappointed you won't live to see the chopped-off heads of your darling fiancé and peasant soldiers held aloft on pikes."

Morgan slashed with inhuman speed. Arthur's instincts and training took over his conscious mind, blocking her attacks with his shield and attacking with Excalibur, which felt weightless in his hand. The clang of blade against blade was as loud as a blacksmith forging steel.

Kate was so tense she forgot to breathe, then had to gasp for air. She could hardly restrain herself from riding out to fight alongside Arthur.

He thrust Excalibur with such force that it knocked Morgan's sword from her grip. "Haaa!" she yelled and extended her left arm. The golden snake bracelet wrapped around her armor became a live serpent with tropical-fish-brilliant scaly skin. It was five times human size and attacked with bared fangs glowing puss green. That spooked Arthur's horse, making it rear back. The king fell and landed hard. The snake coiled victoriously, then lunged for the kill. Arthur rolled sideways, deftly kicking the reptile's head with his armored foot so hard the dazed serpent collapsed. The king jumped up to plunge Excalibur into the snake's brain.

Morgan leaped off her horse, and when her feet touched the ground, she transformed into six knights in identical black armor. They attacked, and when the king sliced one from helmet to torso, there was only magic inside. *Which apparition is Morgan?*

Kate pulled out her sword, but Lancelot held her horse's bridle. "Arthur made an oath to fight knight against knight. We cannot interfere."

"The queen of darkness has sworn no oath of chivalry, and she's turned herself into six! So it's no longer single combat."

Kate pushed his hand off the reins and galloped forward.

Arthur heard cutting metal first, then pain exploded in his shoulder as a blade cut through his armor.

*Endure the pain. Kiba dachi.* He fought on, slicing off the attacker's head, but this wasn't the sorceress. He spun around and around, dodging sword thrusts and parrying others. Each strike on an opponent's blade sparked a fiery stream illuminating the weapons' arcs. Again, he was wounded, this time on his head. Blood dripped into his eyes, blurring his vision. He spun wildly, flailing at his opponents, not knowing exactly where they were.

Kate quickly dismounted.

"Go back!" he yelled.

"This is the 'till death us do part!' part."

They fought back-to-back. A black-armored knight wounded Kate's sword arm, but she was so pumped up with adrenaline that she didn't feel pain, continuing to slash and thrust. Then Arthur smelled the odor of silphium that oozed from Morgan like sweat. At the same time, Kate sensed which knight was the sorceress. They both spun and attacked. Arthur cut a knight's thigh, and Kate wounded his shoulder. The warrior fell to the ground, and the helmet's visor popped open to reveal the sorceress. As her empowering blood gushed from her wounds and her sorcery faded, her flaming hair dulled, and the remaining ghost knights vanished into the summer breeze.

Arthur and Kate pressed the tips of their swords on Morgan's exposed throat, and the king banished the false queen from Camelot and all of England.

# CHAPTER 28

TO CELEBRATE THE ROYAL WEDDING, the gigantic great hall at Castle Camelot was decorated with bright flowers and colorful cloth banners that stretched overhead from wall to wall.

The guests moved to the sides as crowned Arthur and Kate danced to a lilting song played by a band with a lute, fiddle, flute, and tambourine. It amused her how much he liked the accessories. His puffy jacket, cloak, and tight-fitting leggings were like the other men's but embroidered with more gold and finer ermine trimming.

Kate was surprised that she was not astonished how regal Arthur had become. He was not arrogant or demanding but definitely in control as he decided which noble he would grant a private conversation and consulted with the chamberlain, who was in charge of the castle staff, to ensure the celebration ran smoothly.

The couple appeared to be totally absorbed in one another as they danced. But as the king and queen, they both performed as royalty and were alert to the demeanor of their guests to detect any treachery or resentment for the teenage king.

"They never take their eyes off us," he whispered.

"Get used to it. They'll try to spot ways to curry favor or exploit indecision."

"I was certain they were jealous of how beautiful you look."

She grinned. "You're going to do okay at this king thing."

Kate did look glamorous in a gown that glowed brightly in the semi-dark, candle-and torchlit hall. The sparkle of her grandmother's sapphire set in her mother's gold wedding ring matched the exhilaration in her eyes. But, unlike every other lady, she did not wear a close-fitting cloth wimple to cover the blond hair that flowed over her shoulders. And she detected a few noble ladies murmuring their disapproval.

Lancelot stood behind the nobles in the shadows and fixated on Kate. When she looked in his direction, only then did he turn away. He had not drunk wine or mead, so he had control over his desires. But just the sight of her awakened the ache in his heart. He was certain this longing would never die, and it saddened him that he would always have to worship the king's wife from afar.

Arthur beckoned the nobles to join Kate and him. The men formed one line and the women another to dance the estampie. Several ladies curtsied to the queen, then demonstrated elaborate moves, which Kate quickly mastered. But Arthur's gazelle-like grace on the battlefield deserted him on the dance floor, and he kept stumbling over his feet.

Other nobles and their wives watched from long wooden tables, flush-faced from too much wine. The celebration had been going on since the noon ceremony, and there were many yawns. Edmund sat by himself enjoying a venison pie, but his watchful eyes rarely left the king and queen. Not far from him on the table surfaces, dogs gnawed half-eaten legs of mutton and ox ribs thicker than a man's arm. Rats scurried underneath.

A harsh wind with no apparent source gusted through the hall, snuffing out candles and torches, leaving the space dimly lit.

Kate sensed evil. "Morgan!"

A stain-glassed window decorated with the king's three crimson griffins shattered. Morgan appeared on the sill, pulled out a pistol crudely forged by a loyal armorer, and fired. The explosion boomed off the stone walls, eliciting frightened cries. Morgan quickly reloaded by jamming a round bullet into the barrel and inserted black gunpowder that she had concocted after memorizing the ingredients found on the internet while in New York.

Then, with the wind fluttering her robes and swirling her hair into angry snakes, she theatrically descended on a spider's thread. Lancelot sprinted forward to grab her, but she pointed a finger, freezing him into a statue. Edmund got up from the table and moved stealthily toward Arthur and Kate.

"Leave my castle this instant," Arthur commanded, reaching for Excalibur at his side. A spider shot out of Morgan's snake bracelet on her forearm and spun around and around Arthur, pinning his arms to his side with its silk. Kate grabbed her dagger but Morgan waved an arm and the weapon flew from the queen's hand, skittering across the stone floor.

"I don't see how you can enforce that order now, demi-brother. Oh, the irony of having Excalibur so near and so useless against my magic bullet. And Kate, you should have worn black to your wedding because it's also the day of his death!"

Morgan aimed, and Kate yelled, "No!" The sorceress fired, and smoke exploded from the barrel. Only Edmund could see the bullet speeding toward Arthur's forehead. The squire pointed a finger, and the projectile arced upward at the last second to slam against a stone wall.

Edmund then transformed into Merlin, who was once again an ancient man dressed in a flowing robe and peaked cap. A salamander poked its lizard head out of one of his many pockets.

Arthur was stunned and relieved, having no idea how to defeat Morgan. Kate smiled. She wasn't shocked to see the wizard and nodded to herself. Now what she had been sensing but not understanding made sense.

"So you've come back to protect your precious king-e-poo," Morgan sneered at Merlin.

"No. To enforce your banishment."

Morgan turned her right arm into a huge sword. "We'll see about—"

"I never teach an apprentice all my tricks," Merlin said and waved his hand. Morgan zoomed upward, screeching her inhuman birdcall and thrashing ineffectively against his power. Just as she reached the broken window, a shooting star streaked across the sky and sucked the screaming sorceress out of the year 773.

Servants relit candles and torches, and stunned guests looked around. No one was injured. Almost in unison, they sighed in relief. Merlin unfroze Lancelot, who appeared a bit dazed.

Kate gave Merlin a tight hug. "I sensed your presence but couldn't see you, so I didn't trust those feelings. You were the yellow jacket wasp that time-traveled with us, and then you shape-changed into Edmund to keep a watchful eye on your newbie time travelers."

"You had to succeed with your wits and strengths. But your mission is so important to England and history that I couldn't risk not accompanying you."

If anyone besides Kate provided Arthur with advice and wisdom, it was Merlin. Now the king had someone to confirm or challenge what action or decision he was about to make, and to show his respect, he bowed his head. Just a bit.

Then, the king announced, "We welcome our honored guest, Merlin. Morgan Le Fay has not ruined our wedding celebration. Come dance, eat, drink." The king motioned for the band to play. Kate grabbed Merlin's hand and pulled him into the formal dance. But the uninhibited wizard was not constrained by custom or propriety. As the musicians picked up the tempo, he swirled and gyrated more like a teenager at a rock concert than a 140-year-old wizard. Kate joined him, then pulled Arthur into their swirling eddy. The astonished nobles and ladies stood to one side with mixed expressions of disapproval and enjoyment.

The celebration lasted long into the night, but no guests would leave before the king and queen departed—except for Lancelot, who found it unsettling to watch the woman he idolized dance like a wild Pict priestess.

Excited from dancing and wine, Kate whispered something to Arthur. He smiled and offered her his arm as they exited the party. The nobles and ladies bowed and curtsied as the royal couple went by. Merlin didn't even notice their departure as he devoured a venison pie.

At a grand staircase, Arthur started to climb, but Kate grabbed his hand, tugging him in another direction. "Our royal chambers are up—" She put a finger over his lips. "Let's go." He shrugged and laughed to himself. Already the queen commanded.

Ten soldiers with long pikes guarded Camelot's open front gate, and they stood at attention when the king and queen went out into the countryside. Kate started to run, and Arthur chased her, picking up the pace as if they were racing their moonlit shadows. Kate stopped running and pushed through dense underbrush, leading him to an open area. "Our love nest," she sighed, pulling him down next to her onto a bed of soft moss.

The night sounds were soothing: doves cooing, cicadas softly chirping. In the castle, the air was often heavy with the stink of stale sweat and sewage from the moat. Here, it was summer-night fresh, with a trace of honeysuckle. Arthur looked up. "There are so many more bright stars in the seventh century."

"Same stars, only their brilliance is not dimmed by the ambient light of a city or town."

"You're the one who's brilliant for thinking of this."

"You sweet-talking me, Mr. King?"

"Yes ... and I have figured out why we're not resting on a royal mattress of goose feathers with fine royal sheets. You brought me to a bed of moss like we had in Central Park to be sure I won't forget my humble dishwashing origins."

"Don't be ridiculous, Your Gilded and Ermined Majesty." Back in our secret meeting place in Central Park, you missed an opportunity. She opened her arms and whispered, "Come here, my royal husband, I've waited twelve centuries for this moment."

**The End**

# EPILOGUE

CROW WAS PAGING THROUGH *Vogue* on a department store rooftop in present-day New York City when a ball of light descended from the night sky and exploded nearby. Morgan stepped out of the flames, exhaling happily like she had just returned to her cherished home after visiting aunts who crocheted. "What's up, Crow?"

"You again. Can't you get a good haircut in the seventh century?"

"Since Arthur took over, everyone's being so sicky-sweet."

"Well, if it's treachery you're looking for, you'll find plenty of that and more in the New York City commercial real estate business."

"Superb. We'll start by shopping below for stylish outfits suitable for the Skyscraper Queen."

"Caw!"

# AFTERWORD

## WAS THERE A REAL
## KING ARTHUR?

MOST ACADEMICS STUDYING ancient British do not consider King Arthur a historical figure. The character possibly originated in Welsh mythology, appearing as a great warrior defending Britain from human and supernatural enemies. The legendary king largely became a figure of international interest through the popularity of Geoffrey of Monmouth's fanciful and imaginative twelfth-century *Historia Regum Britanniae* (*History of the Kings of Britain*). Geoffrey depicted Arthur as a savior who defeated the invading Saxons from North Central Europe and then established a vast empire within England. Many elements and incidents that are now an integral part of the Arthurian story appear in *Historia*, including Arthur's father Uther Pendragon, the magician Merlin, Arthur's wife Guinevere, the magical sword Excalibur, the king's death in battle against his illegitimate son Mordred, and burial at Avalon. A twelfth-century French writer added Lancelot, the search for the Holy Grail, and romance. In these stories, the narrative often shifts from King Arthur to other characters, such as the Knights of the Round Table, The Green Knight, and Lancelot's and Guinevere's love affair.

Arthurian literature thrived in the Middle Ages and waned in the following centuries until it experienced a major resurgence in the nineteenth century. In the twenty-first century, the legend continues to have prominence in literature, theater, film, television, comics, and other media. The themes, events, and personalities of the Arthurian legend vary widely from text to text, and writers, musicians, playwrights, and filmmakers have implanted their values, and those of their eras, in these legendary figures. I join that list.

# ACKNOWLEDGMENTS

WRITING A BOOK IS OFTEN A LONG and sometimes arduous journey. Many people helped me along the way, providing guidance, sustenance, encouragement, and criticism. This includes my family—Nina, Sophia, Jake, Julia, and Michael, and brothers Steve and George; great and loyal friends—Peter, Jane, and Tina; my fellow writers at the Delray Beach Library Writers' Studio and the Writers' Studio that meets at the wonderful Old Lyme library; and two extraordinary, talented editors who helped me bang the dents out of the story and the manuscript—Emma Dryden and Cheryl Jaclin Isaac. To all, I have heartfelt gratitude.

# About the Author

JONATHAN DAY began his career writing episodic television shows for major networks and selling screenplays to top Hollywood studios. Transitioning into fiction, he has since authored a captivating trilogy: *Sebastian and the Mighty Token*, *Sebastian and the Go-Kart Girl*, and *Sebastian and the Character Hacker*. The series follows Sebastian, a New York City chess-playing computer whiz, as he navigates the complexities of adolescence. Through challenges both humorous and harrowing, Sebastian learns to overcome obstacles that echo the struggles of many young teens. With each novel, Sebastian's world grows richer and more nuanced, as the stakes and consequences in his life deepen alongside his journey into young adulthood.

Jonathan, his wife, daughters, and their families live in and love New York City.

For more information, visit his website, jonathandayauthor.com.